The title of this book reflects my attitude to cooking—and eating. Food and film are my passions and I approach them both with a sense of excitement and adventure.

I was born in an Indian Muslim household. In India, food is very much connected with religious rituals, particularly among Hindus. Every festival and ceremony includes food in one way or another. So, too, cooking and eating are important rituals in Indian daily life.

In this book I introduce some of my new recipes and create others. Some are variations on traditional Indian food, some are classic Indian recipes mostly from the Punjab in northern India, and some are simple light dishes with very distinctive flavors. Some have no connection with India whatsoever— in order to provide choices and variety to the reader, who will never, I hope, labor too hard or too long on following these recipes.

—Ismail Merchant

ISMAIL MERCHANT is one half of the acclaimed film production team Merchant/Ivory. Together with James Ivory, he has produced the award-winning movies *A Room with a View*, *Howards End*, *The Remains of the Day*, and the forthcoming *Golden Bowl*. Born in India, Merchant is an avid lifelong cook.

ISMAIL MERCHANT'S PASSIONATE MEALS

The New Indian Cuisine for Fearless Cooks and Adventurous Eaters

by

Ismail Merchant

Foreword by Madhur Jaffrey

A PLUME BOOK

For Baji, Amina, Safia, Rashida, Sahida and Rukhsana

PLUME
Published by the Penguin Group
Penguin Putnam Inc., 375 Hudson Street, New York, New York 10014, U.S.A.
Penguin Books Ltd, 27 Wrights Lane, London W8 5TZ, England
Penguin Books Australia Ltd, Ringwood, Victoria, Australia
Penguin Books Canada Ltd, 10 Alcorn Avenue, Toronto, Ontario, Canada M4V 3B2
Penguin Books (N.Z.) Ltd, 182–190 Wairau Road, Auckland 10, New Zealand

Penguin Books Ltd, Registered Offices: Harmondsworth, Middlesex, England

Published by Plume, a member of Penguin Putnam Inc.
Originally published by Hyperion.

First Plume Printing, January 2001
10 9 8 7 6 5 4 3 2 1

All photos by Derrick Santini with the exception of those in the first
photo section, which are by Michael Fredericks.

 REGISTERED TRADEMARK—MARCA REGISTRADA

CIP data is available.
Plume ISBN: 0-452-28232-2

Printed in the United States of America
Design by Joel Avirom.

Contents

Foreword by
MADHUR JAFFREY

*I*smail loves to throw parties. A shrewd horse-trader by instinct, parties have always been for him an ideal setting to convince the doubtful, charm the frosted, cajole those holding back, reward the underpaid, and, almost as a by-product, inject a sense of easy camaraderie between those high up in the entertainment establishment and those barely on the rise.

He does this all with the aid of food. Ismail cooks easily and he cooks well. He cooks in swift strokes, with just a hint of perspiration on his forehead. The shopping bags usually come in with him just a few minutes before the guests. This requires both courage and gall, qualities Ismail has in abundance.

The guests in the old days, a good thirty years ago, would be the same mix that you will find in his house today: stars—then they might have been Lauren Bacall, Shirley MacLaine, and Alan Arkin—together with some noted film critic who needed wooing and some humble assistant editors or envelope-stuffers who needed consoling.

The food in those days, when money was scarcer, would consist of chicken legs cooked in yogurt, Indian split peas with lemon (there is a more elaborate version of the dish in this book, Nimbu Masoor Dal), rice, either plain or with peas, and a green salad. On a particularly lavish day or when Ismail had the time to peel and devein them, the electric frying pan in the kitchen would hold shrimp instead of the chicken.

Jim—James Ivory—would clear his well-patinated antique writing table of papers and lay out the knives and forks. The cutlery was generally of top caliber, real silver which had come from Jim's more affluent family. In the living room of the one-bedroom apartment, there were, besides the writing/buffet table, a pair of Indian-Victorian love seats bought from Thieves Market in Bombay, a few assorted chairs, a chest of drawers, and, of course, the enticing aroma of Ismail's food. As Ismail served his guests and the guests took their first bite, he invariably said, "Isn't it wonderful?" even before they could, just as he does at the screening of his movies, an easy charm flowing from every pore. Of course, the food was wonderful.

Today, decades later and after many successful films, the entertaining is done in a large mansion in the country. The mansion, a decrepit hulk when first bought but with fine patrician bones that only Jim could see, has been reclaimed and restored, room by grand room, over the last twenty years. The meals, while sometimes going back to the familiar chicken legs cooked with yogurt, now might well include whole baked legs of lamb, stuffed fish, saffron rice, and the best champagne. Potted orchids grace the drawing room and an Agra carpet stretches out under the federal dining table. In spite of all this, the food at heart has simple, honest tastes and flavors. Ismail has a good palate, hates waste, and cooks, in the last analysis, to please himself. It is a good way to cook. It pleases his guests as well.

Ismail grumbles these days about getting older and threatens to find a Tibetan couple to live in and prepare the meals. I cannot see that happening. Who else can pick up seasonal asparagus from the local farm stand, steam it, dress it with a cayenne and mustard-laced vinaigrette, and have it on the table, all within ten minutes? In India we say that the ability to create flavor is in the hands. Some people just have it. Ismail certainly does.

Foreword by Madhur Jaffrey

The Taste You Create

The title of this book reflects my attitude to cooking—and eating. Food and film are my passions and I approach them both with a sense of excitement and adventure. I consider myself qualified to write a book for Fearless Cooks not only because I am self-taught but also because I disobey all the conventions and laws of cooking, preferring to improvise and make new discoveries all the time. As a cook, you know that cooking is a continuous process that never stops. The invention of new recipes is, for me, the excitement of cooking, and in the kitchen I am always in a creative mood. And as I love to entertain and cook for friends I can truthfully brag that each new recipe has been specially created for this particular occasion. So my guests never feel that they are eating from a standard repertoire, but that something special and new has been made just for them, even if it is only a slight variation on an existing recipe.

The most important element of cooking is the taste you create. My mother used to say that taste was in your hands, in the way you cook with your hands, and it was inborn and could not be acquired. I remember a friend who would invite me to dinner and always use the recipes from the books of the finest chefs and would be very proud of the results, but the food never had any taste. So perhaps my mother was right. On the other hand, no one who has used my recipes has ever complained that the results lack taste.

These days people seem more concerned with the presentation rather than the taste of the food. Beautiful serving dishes, and flower petals as a garnish, are all very fine, but they don't compensate for tasteless food.

The most important part of cooking is to satisfy the taste buds and give the stomach what it yearns for. One of the things I have observed is that when people are served a good meal, no matter how interesting or extraordinary a conversation they are having, all conversation stops. Everything becomes very silent, very still, and all you can hear, even from the most sophisticated people who normally would never make a sound when they eat, is involuntary murmurs of pleasure. At that moment, even greater than the pleasure the meal is giving the guests is the satisfaction of the person who has prepared the food. To be able to achieve that is a great accomplishment.

I was born in an Indian Muslim household. Our diet mainly featured nonvegetarian food. There were some special vegetable dishes which were cooked from time to time, like peas and potatoes, spinach and onions, and string beans with mint, but these were dishes to accompany meat or fish, with less importance given to them than to the rice and the dal (lentil stew) which are the staples of every Indian meal. Nevertheless, I remember these dishes fondly; they have become part of my own repertoire, and I give them greater emphasis now that more people are adopting a vegetarian diet. I hope I have improved on some of these traditional Indian recipes in creating my own, modifying them with the addition of different vegetables available in the West.

I know a famous Bengali writer, Nirad Chaudhri—in fact, we made a film about him—who claims to have started his literary career at the age of fifty only after he changed from a vegetarian diet to a nonvegetarian, becoming a real meat eater. In India vegetarians, who are in the majority, make all kinds of contrasting claims. They feel that not only is meat destructive to life but it inflames the baser passions and inhibits the growth of virtue. There are some sects who go as far as eliminating garlic, beetroot, and even onions from their diet, as being too inflaming. I avoid this sort of extremism and prefer to enjoy everything with which God has provided man to relish.

In India, food is very much connected with religious rituals, particularly among Hindus. Every festival and ceremony includes food in one way or another. One always appears before a deity with sweets and flowers, throughout the year, no matter what the season. So, too, cooking and eating are important rituals in Indian daily life. There are migratory groups of wedding cooks who go from place to place to prepare their specialties. Guests at weddings are generally familiar with particular dishes prepared by the itinerant cooks, and guests go to weddings not only to congratulate the bride and groom, but to take part in these "eating rituals" prepared by wandering chefs. I remember as a young boy being taken to a wedding where half the guests left after congratulating the bride and groom, as the rumor in the mandap (a festive tent put up for weddings) was that their favorite chef had failed to show up to prepare the feast.

When I was a student at St Xavier's College in Bombay, I was fortunately popular with my student friends and found myself often invited to these friends' houses for sumptuous feasts. I was particularly fond of going to the house of a fellow student, Harshad Shangani, to eat Gujerati food. Gujerat is a state in India, the birthplace of Mahatma Gandhi. Gujeratis are vegetarian and make the best vegetarian food—distinctive because of its subtlety, and completely different from any other vegetarian food I have ever tasted. The special ingredients in this cooking are poppy seeds, grated coconut, asafetida, and tamarind. For example, green beans chopped in small pieces were prepared with turmeric, cayenne pepper, and asafetida, with a tamarind sauce.

The family of another friend, Narain Jain, had a strict Brahmin cook, and at his house the vegetarian dishes did not include onions or garlic. Nevertheless, this chef prepared dishes with great finesse. Dals in particular were delicious, and were prepared with a lot of ghee (clarified butter), tamarind, asafetida and poppy seeds, and then garnished with cumin seeds and fresh parsley. I was never allowed to come into the kitchen, or to eat a meal with the family. Instead, Narain and I were served at a Western-style dining table. This segregation was because I was a Muslim meat eater. I remember the silver thalis (flat trays) that were brought, with exquisitely fragrant dishes arranged on them, always served in many small bowls. I particularly remember the hot rotis, with melted ghee, and deep-fried puris which accompanied these dishes.

In this book I introduce some of my new recipes and create others.

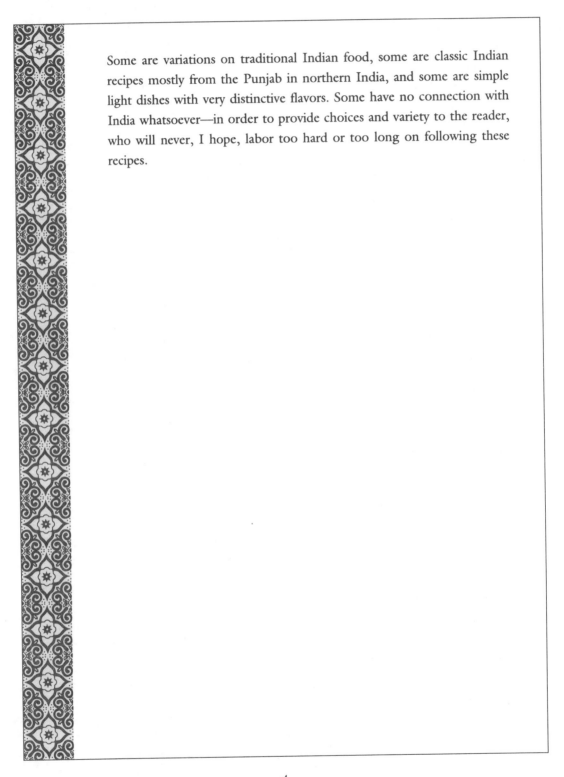

Some are variations on traditional Indian food, some are classic Indian recipes mostly from the Punjab in northern India, and some are simple light dishes with very distinctive flavors. Some have no connection with India whatsoever—in order to provide choices and variety to the reader, who will never, I hope, labor too hard or too long on following these recipes.

A FEW
TIDBITS

In cosmopolitan Indian cities drinking before dinner is very important, to the extent that if you are invited to dine at nine o'clock you are expected to consume hard liquor until the food is served around midnight, by which time you have become so drunk you are incapable of appreciating the dinner that has been prepared. Then at two in the morning you are dragged by your poor wife to your car. You can't drive, of course, so she has to drive if she knows how; otherwise she has to push you and the car home.

For some reason this behavior is considered sophisticated, rather as going to a succession of cocktail parties before dinner is fashionable in the West. But I strongly disapprove of both these customs, because excessive drinking before eating kills those senses that respond to food. A good bloody Mary, a gin and tonic, a Cinzano with a

twist of lemon, or just a glass of wine is fine before dinner, but anything more tires the senses and prohibits the appreciation of the food—and that is an injustice to the chef who has prepared the meal, whether it is in a restaurant or a private home.

Generally, I like to serve some simple hors d'oeuvres with drinks before dinner. It never happens that all the guests arrive at the same time, so a few tidbits served in advance of dinner are always a good idea. That way, no one gets impatient to eat and so there's no need to plunk the food down immediately. You can enjoy a few drinks and a nice conversation without dying of hunger. Some pakoras (savory fritters) and cheese toasts, or just spiced peanuts and fried spiced cashew nuts, set the tone for a leisurely evening.

Ismail Merchant's Passionate Meals

Meethi Lassi
Sweet Lassi

❖

Yogurt, in one form or another, is an essential part of Indian meals. The English word "curry," which has become the generic description of Indian food, derives from an Indian dish called curri, which is made from yogurt and chick-pea flour. Yogurt is used in making korma sauce, with vegetables, and is the basic ingredient of a raita, the yogurt and cucumber accompaniment of every Indian meal.

You can drink lassi before a meal or with the meal, either sweetened or salted. It's very refreshing, and is good for the stomach. Lassi can be flavored with almonds and pistachios, with rose petals and rose water, with cinnamon and cardamom, with nutmeg—there are dozens of variations.

People mostly prefer to drink the sweetened varieties, but salty lassi is good in hot weather.

Preparation time: 10 minutes

Serves 6

3¾ cups plain yogurt
½ cup rose water
¼ cup sugar
1 dozen unsalted pistachios, shelled and coarsely chopped

Whisk the yogurt, rose water, sugar, and chopped pistachios together with 3¾ cups water for 3 to 4 minutes, until the mixture becomes frothy. Serve at room temperature or chilled.

Namkeen Lassi

Salty Lassi

❖

Preparation time: 10 minutes

Serves 6

    3¾ cups plain yogurt
    ½ teaspoon salt
    ½ teaspoon ground cumin

Whisk the yogurt, salt, and cumin together with 3¾ cups of water for 3 to 4 minutes, until the mixture becomes frothy. Correct the seasoning and serve at room temperature or chilled.

A Better Gin and Tonic

Preparation time: 5 minutes

Serves 1

    Ice cubes
    2 ounces superior dry gin
    Juice of ½ lemon or lime, freshly squeezed
    Tonic water
    A slice of lemon or lime, to garnish

Fill a tall glass with ice cubes and add the gin. Stir in the lemon or lime juice and fill the glass with tonic water. Add the lemon or lime slice and serve.

Minted Vodka Tonic

❖

I suggest that this be enjoyed in a hammock. Do not try to navigate after drinking.

Preparation time: 5 minutes

Serves 1

Ice cubes
2 ounces 100 proof vodka
8 to 10 fresh mint leaves
Tonic water OR soda

Fill a large wine goblet with ice cubes and add the vodka. Add the mint leaves, stir them vigorously, fill the glass with tonic water, and serve.

Beer and Lemon for a Hot Afternoon

❖

This is a very satisfying drink for a sultry day.

Preparation time: 5 minutes

Serves 1

Ice cubes
10 ounces lager beer
Juice of ½ lemon, freshly squeezed
A sprig of mint, to garnish

Fill a tall glass with ice, then add the beer. Stir in the lemon juice, insert the mint, and serve.

Dahi
Homemade Yogurt

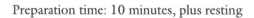

Preparation time: 10 minutes, plus resting

Serves 4–6

2 cups milk
2 teaspoons natural yogurt

Bring the milk to a boil in a saucepan, stirring to prevent a skin from forming, then turn the heat off and let the milk cool until it is tepid. Transfer the milk into a bowl and add the yogurt. Give it a quick whisk in order to blend, then cover the bowl and place it in a warm, dark place such as a cupboard or pantry. Leave it overnight, or for at least 8 hours. Then keep in the refrigerator.

Garam Masala

◆

This is a very common flavoring ingredient added to various Indian dishes.

Preparation time: 5 minutes

Makes 1½ pounds

8 ounces coriander seeds
8 ounces cumin seeds
2 ounces cinnamon sticks
2 ounces black peppercorns
2 ounces black cardamom pods
1 ounce whole cloves
1 tablespoon ground dried ginger

Grind all the ingredients to a fine powder and store in an airtight container. You can use a food processor for this, or a coffee grinder, but only if you have a spare coffee grinder; otherwise your coffee, ground in the same grinder, will have the aroma of the garam masala. This can be stored for a long time.

Vada
Moong Dal (Lentil) Balls

———————————— ◆ ————————————

Preparation time: 15–20 minutes, plus soaking

Makes 16, approximately

¾ pound moong dal (split mung beans)
1½ teaspoons salt
1 fresh hot green chili, cored and seeded
¼ teaspoon ground red pepper
¼ teaspoon ground black pepper
A handful of fresh coriander
Vegetable oil for deep frying

Wash the dal thoroughly and remove any stones. Cover with water and soak for 3 to 4 hours. Drain well and combine with the salt, chili, red and black pepper, and coriander in a food processor. Blend. The mixture should have a thick, creamy consistency after about a minute. If it is too dry, add a tablespoon or two of water. Form into 1- to 1½-inch balls (about 1 heaping teaspoon each).

Heat the oil to 375°F in a deep, heavy pan. Fry the balls in batches for 3 to 5 minutes, turning over once or twice, until lightly browned. Remove with a slotted spoon and drain on paper towels. Serve warm or cold.

Vada Raita

❖

Preparation time: 20 minutes

Serves 4–6

½ teaspoon cumin seeds
12 vada balls (see opposite page)
1 cup plain yogurt
¼ teaspoon ground red pepper
Small handful of fresh coriander leaves

Dry-roast the cumin seeds in a small pan and crush them with a rolling pin or mortar and pestle. Soak the vada balls in enough water to cover for 5 minutes, then squeeze out the water from the balls with your hands. They should not break. Whisk the yogurt to thin it to a saucelike consistency. Add a little milk if it is still too thick.

Combine the red pepper, cumin, and yogurt in a bowl. Add the vada balls and stir gently. Garnish with the coriander.

Kheera ka Raita
Cucumber Raita

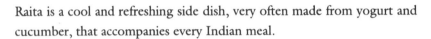

Raita is a cool and refreshing side dish, very often made from yogurt and cucumber, that accompanies every Indian meal.

Preparation time: 5 minutes, plus chilling

Serves 5–6

   1¾ cups plain yogurt
   1 medium cucumber, peeled and grated
   ½ teaspoon salt
   ½ teaspoon ground cumin
   A sprig of mint, chopped

Stir the yogurt with a fork until it is smooth. Stir the cucumber into the yogurt with the salt, cumin, and mint. Chill slightly before serving.

Coconut and Raisin Raita

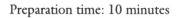

Preparation time: 10 minutes

Serves 4

½ fresh coconut, grated
2 fresh hot green chilies, seeded and chopped fine
1 cup plain yogurt
½ teaspoon sugar
25 golden raisins, halved
Salt to taste
2 tablespoons chopped fresh coriander leaves

Mix all the ingredients well and serve as a relish.

Piston-walla Raita

Pistachio Raita

Preparation time: 5 minutes, plus chilling

Serves 6

  3 cups plain yogurt
  ¼ cup rose water
  2 tablespoons honey
  3 dozen unsalted pistachios, shelled and chopped
  A pinch of ground saffron (optional)

Mix together the yogurt, rose water, and honey. Stir in the pistachios. Chill.

Sprinkle the saffron over the mixture, if desired, and serve.

Raita with Lauki

❖

Lauki, also known as ghiya or kiya, is a vegetable that is available in Indian and Chinese groceries. It is similar to a small marrow (pale green squash), but harder in texture.

Preparation time: 20 minutes, plus chilling

Serves 4–6

¼ pound lauki, peeled and grated
½ teaspoon cumin seeds
2 cups plain yogurt
½ teaspoon salt
Lots of freshly ground black pepper
Pinch of ground red pepper
Handful of chopped fresh coriander leaves

Put the lauki in a small pan and cover with water. Bring to a boil and boil for 10 minutes. Drain and squeeze out all the water. Heat the cumin seeds in a small dry skillet until lightly toasted and crush them lightly with a rolling pin. Combine all the ingredients, reserving the coriander to sprinkle on the top.

Phoodina Raita
Tomato Mint Raita

◆

Preparation time: 5–10 minutes

Serves 4

- 2 medium onions, halved and sliced thin
- 2 medium tomatoes, peeled and sliced thin
- 1 cup plain yogurt
- 3 or 4 fresh mint sprigs, stemmed and chopped
- 1 2-inch piece of fresh hot green chili, seeded (optional) and finely chopped
- ¾ teaspoon ground cumin OR ½ teaspoon ground red pepper, if you prefer it spicier
- ¼ teaspoon salt

Combine the onions and tomatoes with the yogurt.

Add the mint, chili, cumin or red pepper, and salt. Mix well and serve.

Bundi Raita

❖

Preparation time: 30 minutes

Serves 4–6

2 tablespoons besan (chick-pea flour)
Salt
Ground red pepper
Ground black pepper
Vegetable oil for deep frying
1½ cups plain yogurt
2–3 teaspoons milk, or as needed
Crushed roasted cumin seeds

Stir together the flour, ½ teaspoon salt, ¼ teaspoon each of red and black pepper, and 2 tablespoons of water in a bowl to make a batter.

Heat about 2 inches of oil to 375°F in a deep frying pan. Pour the batter through a slotted spoon into the oil. It will form little droplets (the bundi). Fry until golden and remove with a slotted spoon. Drain on paper towels.

Beat the yogurt until smooth and add a little milk to make it runny. Soak 3 tablespoons of the prepared bundi in water for 5 minutes until soft. Squeeze out the water and add them to the yogurt. Season with a little salt, red and black pepper, and a few crushed roasted cumin seeds.

Any leftover bundi not needed for this recipe can be stored in a jar in the refrigerator and served as a snack.

Bambai Bhajya
Bombay Vegetable Fritters

❖

Preparation time: 60 minutes

Serves 6–8

FOR THE BATTER:

    2 teaspoons vegetable oil
    6 ounces besan (chick-pea flour)
    1½ teaspoons salt
    1 teaspoon ground cumin
    1 teaspoon ground coriander
    ½ teaspoon ground red pepper
    1 cup warm water

VEGETABLES:

    1 small cauliflower, cut into bite-size florets
    2 medium onions, thickly sliced and divided into rings
    2 or 3 medium potatoes, boiled until just tender, then cooled under
        cold running water, drained, peeled, and cut into bite-size rounds

Vegetable oil for frying

First, make the batter. Mix the 2 teaspoons of oil into the flour until the oil is evenly absorbed. Mix in the salt, cumin, coriander, and red pepper.

Slowly pour in 1 cup of warm water, beating continuously until the mixture is thin and smooth. (A food processor or a blender does this admirably.) Let the batter stand for about 30 minutes.

Meanwhile, prepare the vegetables. Heat the oil to 375°F in a deep-fat frier or a deep heavy saucepan filled to a depth of about 2 inches. Dip the vegetables into the batter, shaking off the excess, and fry them in batches until they turn golden brown.

Remove fritters with a slotted spoon. Drain them on several thicknesses of paper towels. Serve hot, with toothpicks.

Kali Rai Walla Toasts
Cheese Toasts with Mustard Seeds

❖

Preparation time: 10 minutes

Serves 4–6

8 slices firm white bread
8 ounces Cheddar or any other hard cheese, sliced
Mustard seeds OR cumin seeds
Ground red pepper to taste

Preheat the broiler. Toast the bread very lightly on both sides and place on a baking sheet. Arrange cheese slices so they cover each piece of toast. Sprinkle the cheese with either mustard seeds or cumin seeds and then with red pepper.

Place under medium heat and broil for about 3 minutes, until the cheese melts and browns. If, like me, you are doing other things at the same time and forget the toasts under the broiler, don't panic; just trim the burnt crusts before cutting each toast into quarters.

Pakoras

Preparation time: 40 minutes

Makes 10–12

1¼ pounds red potatoes, peeled and cut into small pieces
1 small cauliflower, chopped into ¼-inch pieces
1 medium eggplant, peeled and chopped into ¼-inch pieces
1 large onion, peeled and finely chopped
1 or 2 fresh hot green chilies, seeded and finely chopped
1 pound spinach leaves, washed and finely chopped
2 cups besan (chick-pea flour)
1 teaspoon ground red pepper
1 teaspoon garam masala (recipe on page 13)
1 tablespoon salt
½ teaspoon ajwain (lovage) seeds
1 tablespoon plain yogurt
Vegetable oil for frying

Put the potatoes, cauliflower, eggplant, onion, chili, and spinach in a large bowl and stir in the flour and seasonings. Add the yogurt and gradually add about 2 cups of water, mixing with your hands to make a loose batter.

Heat the oil to 375°F in a deep frying pan and drop generous tablespoons of the mixture into the oil. Fry the pakoras in batches, turning over once or twice until they are golden brown all over and the vegetables are tender. Remove with a slotted spoon. Drain on paper towels. Serve hot with chutney as a snack. Mint and coriander chutneys are particularly good with these.

Makai ka Pakoras
Fresh Corn Pakoras

Preparation time: 30 minutes

Serves 4

6 ears of fresh corn
1 tablespoon besan (chick-pea flour)
1 teaspoon sugar
¼ teaspoon turmeric
2 tablespoons plain yogurt
1 tablespoon chopped fresh coriander leaves
4 fresh hot green chilies, chopped
A small piece of fresh ginger root, grated
Salt to taste
Vegetable oil for frying

Shuck the corn and cut the kernels off the cobs into a large bowl. Add the besan, sugar, turmeric, yogurt, coriander, chilies, ginger, and salt, stirring until well combined.

Heat about 2 inches of oil to 375°F in a deep heavy pan. Using a large spoon, scoop up about 3 tablespoons of batter and drop it into the hot oil. Fry the pakoras in batches, 5 or 6 at a time, turning over once or twice, until they are light brown. Remove pakoras with a slotted spoon as they are done and drain on paper towels. Serve hot.

Sabzi Pakoras
Mixed Vegetable Pakoras

Preparation time: 40 minutes

Serves 4

1 pound mixed vegetables: cauliflower, carrots, green beans, onions, peppers (see Note)
1 cup besan (chick-pea flour)
1 cup sooji (semolina)
¼ teaspoon turmeric
2 tablespoons plain yogurt
A pinch of asafetida
2 teaspoons sugar
6 fresh hot green chilies, seeded and puréed in a blender
A small piece of fresh ginger root, grated
¼ teaspoon ground red pepper
Salt to taste
Vegetable oil for frying

Peel, wash, and chop all the vegetables fine, then steam or boil them until tender.

Mix together the besan, sooji, turmeric, yogurt, asafetida, sugar, the puréed chilies, ginger, red pepper, salt, and 1 teaspoon of oil. Stir in all the steamed vegetables. Add a little water if required to make a batter that holds together. Form the mixture into small balls.

Heat about 2 inches of oil to 375°F in a deep frying pan. Fry the pakoras in batches, turning over once or twice, until they are golden brown. Remove with a slotted spoon. Drain on paper towels. Serve hot.

NOTE: There is no need to start this recipe by boiling fresh vegetables if your refrigerator contains odd bits of leftovers. Chop enough of them to fill a two-cup measure, or use a combination of the fresh and the already cooked.

Aloo aur Methi ke Pakoras
Potato and Fenugreek Pakoras

❖

Preparation time: 1 hour

Serves 8

1 pound new potatoes, scrubbed
6 fresh hot green chilies, puréed in a blender
A small piece of fresh ginger root, grated
Salt to taste
2 tablespoons arrowroot or rice flour
1 cup plain yogurt OR the juice of 1 lemon
2 teaspoons sugar
2 ounces dried fenugreek leaves, finely chopped
Vegetable oil for frying

Cook the potatoes in boiling water for 20 to 30 minutes or until soft. Peel and mash with a fork, making a smooth pulp. Add the chilies, ginger, salt, arrowroot, yogurt, sugar, and fenugreek. Mix well.

Form the mixture into 20 small balls.

Heat about 2 inches of oil to 375°F in a deep heavy pan. Fry the pakoras in batches, turning over once or twice, until they are light brown. Remove with a slotted spoon. Drain on paper towels. Serve on toothpicks.

Aloo Besan Sev

◆

Sev is a crisp, delicious snack resembling deep-fried vermicelli. It is made in a special gadget manufactured just for that purpose, but a potato ricer may be used instead. You can buy it ready-made, but here is a recipe.

Preparation time: 45 minutes

Serves 4–6

1 pound new or red potatoes, scrubbed
1 cup besan (chick-pea flour)
½ teaspoon ground red pepper
¼ teaspoon asafetida
Salt to taste
Vegetable oil for frying

Cook the potatoes in boiling water for 20 to 30 minutes or until soft. Then peel and mash until smooth. Add the besan, red pepper, asafetida, salt, and 1 teaspoon of oil. Mix well. If required, add a little water to make a workable dough.

Heat about 2 inches of oil in a deep, heavy pan to 375°F. Shape a handful of dough into a ball and place it in the sev mold or in a potato ricer. Hold the device over the hot oil and push the dough through, moving it as necessary to cover the surface of the oil. Fry 1 to 2 minutes, turning once, until a very light brown. Repeat with remaining dough.

Remove the sev with a slotted spoon. Drain on paper towels. When crisp, store in a jar with a tight lid. You may serve immediately or refrigerate for future use.

Kebabs

Preparation time: 20 minutes

Makes 20

6 or 7 garlic cloves, peeled
½ bunch fresh coriander stems and leaves
2½ teaspoons salt
1 fresh hot green chili, seeds removed
1 teaspoon ground red pepper
5 teaspoons garam masala (see page 13)
2-inch piece fresh ginger root, peeled
1 small onion, peeled
1 tablespoon ground roasted chana dal (yellow split peas)
Juice of 2 lemons
2 pounds ground lamb

In the container of a blender or food processor, combine the garlic, coriander, salt, chili, red pepper, garam masala, ginger root, onion, chana dal, and lemon juice. Blend to a smooth paste. Add this to the meat in a large bowl and mix thoroughly with your hands.

Take a small handful and press into hollow sausage shapes around an oiled thin wooden spoon handle. Slide the kebab off the handle and repeat with the rest of the meat. Grill on a barbecue, turning until cooked through, about 5 to 10 minutes. Or cook on a stovetop grill or under a broiler, turning occasionally, for 5 to 10 minutes, or until cooked through. Serve as a snack with sweet or ready-made mango chutney and sliced onions.

THE IMPORTANCE OF SOUPS

It wasn't until I came to America that I discovered the importance of soup as part of a meal, or even as a meal in itself—especially the traditional dumpling soups of China and Russia, the famous Jewish matzo ball soup, and Italian minestrone. A hearty soup needs only some really good bread and a crisp salad to be complete.

Soup is not native to Indian cuisine. The closest Indian equivalents are certain dal and pulse dishes (lentil stews) that are like very thick soups, but served with, rather than before, the rest of the meal. When I was a little boy I remember all the food being brought together on the dining table or the dastar khaun, a mat or special cloth spread on the floor. Soup was usually served only in Western or Westernized households.

Mulligatawny soup (which is very spicy) has somehow or other become associated with Indian food but it is, in fact, very much an English dish both in origin and character. The soup recipes here are my own style, but of course influenced by the spices and flavors of India.

Much as I enjoy soup, if I am cooking for more than six people I rarely make it because of the amount of labor involved. Certainly after working all day one wants to avoid extra burdens when preparing dinner. But when there is time—during weekends at my country house in upstate New York, for example—then making soup isn't a chore at all. In autumn and winter, especially, soup is a wonderful addition to a meal. And even in summer a light soup is nice to have.

Because I don't like laboring over food, all the soup recipes I have created are very simple—unlike the soups my partner, director James Ivory, makes, which involve a whole traditional ritual of chopping and cooking and preparing and taking up hours of time. I just don't have the patience for all that. So, although I can collaborate with Jim on many things, and especially films, we never make a soup together.

Avocado aur Tamatar ka Shorba

Avocado and Tomato Soup

Preparation time: 15 minutes, plus chilling

Serves 2–3

 3 ripe avocados
 1¼ cups vegetable or chicken stock
 ½ cup light cream
 ½ cup tomato puree (see Note)
 1 to 2 teaspoons onion juice, strained
 1½ teaspoons lemon juice, or to taste
 Salt and pepper to taste

Remove the pits and skin from the avocados. Mash the flesh in a large bowl.

Whisk in the stock, cream, tomato purée, onion juice, and lemon juice.

Season with salt, pepper, and more lemon juice, if desired. Chill before serving.

NOTE: If you eliminate the tomato purée you will have a paler and milder-tasting soup. The flavor of the avocados will become more prominent.

Adrak Broccoli Walla Shorba

Ginger Broccoli Soup

❖

Preparation time: 25 minutes

Serves 4

1 tablespoon butter
1 medium onion, halved and sliced thin
3¾ cups chicken stock
1-inch piece fresh ginger root, peeled and grated
Juice of 1 lemon
½ teaspoon ground red pepper
6 ounces fresh tender broccoli tops, cut into bite-size florets

Melt the butter in a saucepan over medium-low heat. Add the onion and cook until it begins to brown, stirring occasionally.

Meanwhile, heat the stock with 2½ cups of water and the grated ginger in a saucepan for 5 or 6 minutes. Do not boil.

Add the onion, lemon juice, red pepper, and broccoli to the liquid. Simmer, stirring occasionally, for 7 minutes. Do not let the soup boil. Serve right away.

Claverack ka Khas Gajar Shorba

Claverack Carrot Soup

❖

This is a variation of the classic French carrot soup, potage Crécy. Instead of rice, potatoes are used as a thickener, along with a generous amount of onion. Fresh ginger adds the distinctive flavor.

Preparation time: about 1 hour

Serves 4–6

4 tablespoons (½ stick) unsalted butter
1 pound carrots, peeled and thinly sliced
1 large onion, peeled and chopped
2 large baking potatoes, peeled and coarsely diced
2-inch piece of fresh ginger root, peeled and grated (see Note)
3¾ cups chicken stock
1¼ cups light cream
Salt to taste

Melt half the butter in a small pan over low heat. Add the carrots, stir, cover, and cook until they soften, stirring occasionally.

Meanwhile, melt the rest of the butter in a large saucepan over low heat. Add the onion and cook until it is soft, stirring occasionally. Remove the pan from the heat.

Add the carrots, with the pan juices, to the onions. Add the potatoes, ginger, and chicken stock. Bring the mixture to a boil, reduce the heat, and simmer for 30 minutes.

Stir the cream into the hot soup. If the soup is too thick, add a little water or stock. Season with salt to taste.

NOTE: As the ginger creates a tangy flavor, pepper is not necessary. For those who particularly like ginger, double the amount.

Hindustani Gazpacho
Indian Gazpacho

❖

One can make gazpacho out of all sorts of things. Virtually any raw vegetable will do, provided it has some crispness. Here is a very tangy version that requires no cooking.

Preparation time: 20 minutes, plus chilling

Serves 6

6 large tomatoes
1 large onion, preferably red
1 large green or red bell pepper, seeded
2 bunches of radishes, trimmed
3 large carrots, peeled
3 large celery stalks, trimmed
2 medium-size cucumbers, unpeeled
2 fresh hot green chilies, seeded if desired
6 to 8 large garlic cloves, peeled
2 tablespoons olive oil
About ½ cup of tomato purée
5¼ cups chicken stock
1¾ cups dry red wine
Salt to taste

Blanch and skin the tomatoes and chop them coarsely. Cut the onion, bell pepper, radishes, carrots, celery, and cucumbers into small chunks. Mix the vegetables in a bowl with the chilies, garlic, olive oil, tomato purée, chicken stock, and wine.

Process the mixture in batches in a food processor or blender. Make sure there aren't any chunks of unprocessed vegetables, but do not let the soup become too thin. Season with salt. Chill before serving.

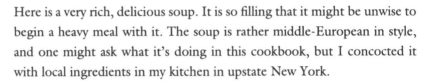

Taza Kumbhi ka Shorba
Fresh Mushroom Soup

Here is a very rich, delicious soup. It is so filling that it might be unwise to begin a heavy meal with it. The soup is rather middle-European in style, and one might ask what it's doing in this cookbook, but I concocted it with local ingredients in my kitchen in upstate New York.

Preparation time: about 1 hour

Serves 6

> 4 to 6 tablespoons butter
> 1 large onion, peeled and chopped
> 1 pound button mushrooms, sliced
> 1¼ cups dry red or white wine (I prefer red)
> 3¾ cups chicken stock
> 1¾ cups heavy cream
> A small bunch of fresh parsley, finely chopped

Melt 2 tablespoons of the butter in a small frying pan over medium-low heat. Add the onion and cook for 2 or 3 minutes, stirring frequently. It should not become too soft. Remove from the heat.

Heat another 2 tablespoons of the butter in a large saucepan over medium-low heat. Add the mushrooms and cook for 8 or 10 minutes, adding more butter as needed. When the mushrooms are soft, add the wine and cook for 5 more minutes.

Add the chicken stock and onion to the mushrooms and simmer gently for 15 minutes over a low flame. Do not let the mixture boil.

Ismail Merchant's Passionate Meals

Process the mixture in batches in a food processor or blender until almost puréed; a few pieces should remain.

When ready to serve, reheat the mushroom mixture. Turn the heat to low and stir in the cream. When hot but not boiling, serve the soup garnished with a sprinkling of parsley.

Masoor Dal Shorba
Red Lentil Soup

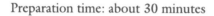

Preparation time: about 30 minutes

Serves 6

3 tablespoons vegetable oil
1 medium onion, peeled and chopped
12 peppercorns
4 bay leaves
3¾ cups chicken stock
1 cup masoor dal (red lentils), picked over, washed, and drained
2 tablespoons chopped fresh parsley
3 dried red chilies, seeded (optional)
Salt
A ¼- to ½-inch piece of fresh ginger root, grated

Heat the oil in a saucepan over low heat. Add the onion and cook until it begins to soften, about 5 minutes, stirring occasionally.

Add the peppercorns and bay leaves and cook for an additional 5 minutes.

Add the chicken stock, 1 cup of water, the drained lentils, parsley, chilies, and salt to taste. Cook over medium heat, stirring occasionally, for 10 minutes.

When the soup begins to boil, add the grated ginger. Continue cooking for another 10 minutes, or until the lentils are very soft. Remove the bay leaves before serving.

Aloo aur Hari Pati ka Shorba

Potato Watercress Soup

❖

Preparation time: about 1¼ hours

Serves 6

    4 large red potatoes
    4 tablespoons (½ stick) butter
    2 medium onions, peeled and chopped
    3¾ cups chicken stock
    4 large garlic cloves, peeled and minced
    1 to 1½ teaspoons ground white pepper
    1 bunch of watercress, stems removed
    2½ cups milk
    Salt to taste

Boil the potatoes, with the skins on or off, as you prefer, until very tender, 25 to 30 minutes. The skins are healthy and good, and the soup will look agreeably speckled if you leave them on. Drain the potatoes and cut into chunks.

Meanwhile, melt the butter in a large saucepan over low heat. Add the onions and cook until they are softened but do not color, about 8 to 10 minutes. Remove from the heat.

Add the chicken stock to the onions, with the garlic, potatoes, and pepper. Bring to a simmer and cook for 25 minutes. Sprinkle the watercress on top of the simmering liquid—do not mix in—and continue cooking for another 5 minutes.

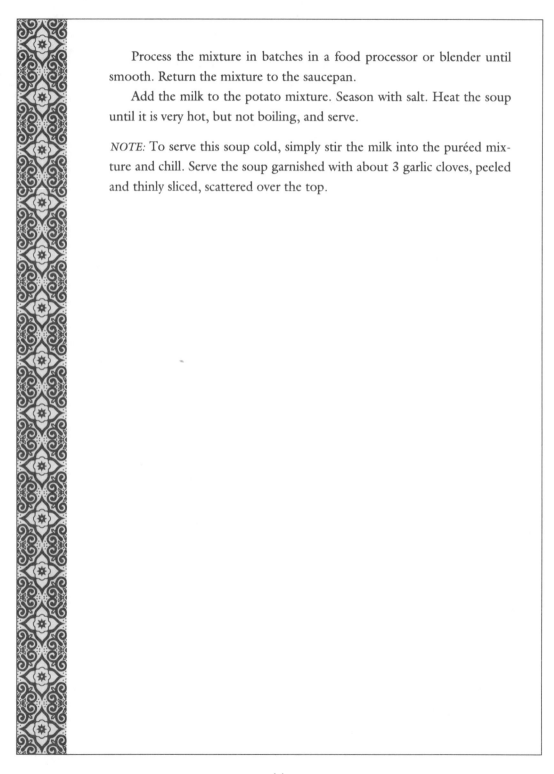

Process the mixture in batches in a food processor or blender until smooth. Return the mixture to the saucepan.

Add the milk to the potato mixture. Season with salt. Heat the soup until it is very hot, but not boiling, and serve.

NOTE: To serve this soup cold, simply stir the milk into the puréed mixture and chill. Serve the soup garnished with about 3 garlic cloves, peeled and thinly sliced, scattered over the top.

TWO HUGE LETTUCES

In India, salad is not commonly eaten with meals. In fact, fresh crunchy vegetables and greenstuffs are hardly ever served in that state. But since I came to America, salads have become very important in my kitchen and they accompany almost every meal.

The first time I returned to Bombay, in 1961, the family prepared a wonderful biryani with basmati rice, but I thought we should also have some salad. So I left all the guests sitting there and rushed to Crawford Market to buy two huge lettuces. I took them home, washed and dried them, and made a dressing with oil, lemon juice, and mustard. At first none of the family or the guests were keen to try my salad because it wasn't what they were used to. But I begged them to taste it and from that time salad became a must with every meal.

One of the best and simplest salads consists only of a good lettuce, properly washed and dried, then chilled, and dressed with a superior olive oil, a little salt, and some fresh lemon juice. It never fails. Don't forget to toss any mixed or dressed salad very thoroughly.

Gazar Salaad
Carrot Salad

Preparation time: 15 minutes

Serves 4–5

  1 cup grated carrots
  1 heaping teaspoon Dijon mustard
  ¼ cup olive oil
  1½ tablespoons herb vinegar
  ¼ teaspoon ground red pepper (optional)

Put the grated carrots into a serving bowl. To make the dressing, put the mustard into a small bowl, add the oil and mix with a fork, then add the vinegar and the red pepper, if desired. Mix very well, then pour the dressing over the carrots and toss until the carrots are coated with the dressing.

Seerke-walli Saljam
Beets Vinaigrette

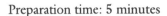

Preparation time: 5 minutes

Serves 4

  2 tablespoons vegetable oil
  2 tablespoons tarragon vinegar
  1 tablespoon chopped fresh parsley
  A pinch of salt
  A pinch of ground red pepper
  6 medium beets, boiled, peeled, and sliced

Stir together the oil, vinegar, parsley, salt, and red pepper. Pour the mixture over the beets and serve.

Chuqandar Monesh
Monesh Beets

I prepared this salad at a lunch I gave for Monesh Mohan, a Manhattan restaurateur, who wanted to use some of my recipes at a new restaurant he was opening in the city. I was surprised and delighted to discover that the beet is one of his favorite foods.

Preparation time: 1¼ hours

Serves 4–6

3 large beets
3 garlic cloves, peeled and sliced
1 teaspoon black mustard seeds
¼ cup virgin olive oil
1 tablespoon vinegar

Cook the beets in boiling water to cover for about 1 hour, or until tender. Cool, then peel and slice into rounds. Put in a bowl and add the garlic and mustard seeds. Mix the oil and vinegar, pour over the beets, and serve.

Safaid Patte Akhroot ka Salaad

Endive-Walnut Salad

Preparation time: 5 minutes

Serves 2

> 3 or 4 heads of Belgian endive
> A handful of chopped walnuts
> 2 tablespoons walnut oil
> 2 tablespoons tarragon vinegar
> A pinch of salt

Cut the endives into bite-size pieces and put them in a salad bowl.

Mix the rest of the ingredients together, toss them with the endive, and serve.

NOTE: One or two garlic cloves, peeled and crushed, are an excellent addition to the dressing, as the flavor of garlic is delicious with walnuts.

Sukhi Pati Akhroot aur Aloo ka Salaad

Tarragon-Walnut Potato Salad

Preparation time: 30 minutes, plus chilling

Serves 8–10

- 5 pounds small potatoes, preferably red, scrubbed
- 1 cup mayonnaise
- ½ cup Dijon mustard
- ¼ cup walnut oil
- 2 tablespoons tarragon vinegar
- 4 or more large sprigs of fresh dill, chopped
- ½ teaspoon salt
- ½ teaspoon ground red pepper
- 2 medium-size onions, peeled and chopped

Cook the potatoes in their skins in boiling water for 20 to 25 minutes, or until they are just tender.

Meanwhile, mix together the mayonnaise, mustard, oil, vinegar, dill, salt, and red pepper. Stir in the onions.

Refresh the potatoes under cold running water for 2 or 3 minutes, drain well, and cut them in half lengthwise.

Gently toss the potatoes with the mayonnaise mixture. Cover and refrigerate until ready to serve.

Palak Salaad
Raw Spinach Salad

Preparation time: 5–10 minutes

Serves 4

    3 tablespoons olive oil
    2 tablespoons tarragon vinegar
    2 tablespoons capers, chopped
    1½ teaspoons salt
    1 pound spinach, washed, stems removed, and dried
    1 large onion, preferably red, peeled and sliced thin

Make the dressing by combining the oil, vinegar, capers, and salt. Just before serving, pour the dressing over the spinach and sliced onion. Toss thoroughly and serve.

VARIATION: Another very good dressing for this simple salad is made by combining the juice of 1 large lemon, 3 tablespoons of olive oil, and 2 tablespoons of prepared spicy mustard.

Mirch aur Tamatur ka Salaad

Chili-Tomato Salad

Preparation time: 5 minutes, plus chilling

Serves 2

12 cherry tomatoes OR 6 small tomatoes
½ bunch parsley, stemmed and chopped
½ fresh hot green chili, seeded (optional) and chopped
1 teaspoon Dijon mustard
1½ teaspoons vegetable oil
2 tablespoons lemon juice
A pinch of salt
A pinch of ground red pepper

Halve the cherry tomatoes, or quarter the small tomatoes.

Mix the chopped parsley and chili with the tomatoes in a small serving bowl and chill.

Combine the mustard, oil, lemon juice, salt, and red pepper for the dressing, and reserve.

Add the dressing to the chilled tomatoes just before serving.

A FRESH WAVE OF VEGETABLES

In every market in Bombay, from the smallest to the largest, you will always find a plentiful supply of vegetables. This is partly because most Indians are vegetarians and partly because vegetables are inexpensive, so those people who cannot afford meat or fish are always able to buy something.

I used to go to Crawford Market in Bombay, which had every kind of native vegetable and also imported varieties that you couldn't find anywhere else. Westernized

Ismail Merchant's Passionate Meals

Indians and European memsahibs would go to Crawford Market for avocados, brussels sprouts, lettuces, and so on, which were as exotic to India as chilies and ginger used to be to London or New York. Sometimes I would go there with my close friend Jennifer Kendal, a fine actress who appeared in several of our films including <u>Bombay Talkie</u> and <u>Heat and Dust</u>. She was a vegetarian, and we would discover the most wonderful things to buy. Even so, I never saw an artichoke until I went to England.

The house where I grew up was just a few hundred steps from Nul Bazaar, which was also very good, but there was no other place like Crawford Market. It was not just the varieties of vegetables that were available there but also the stylish and systematic way they were presented. All the stalls were decorated, and piled high with huge pyramids of lemons and eggplants, carrots, potatoes, and onions. The vegetables were always very fresh, brought to the market early in the morning, and usually everything was sold by eleven o'clock. So in the evening there would be a fresh wave of vegetables. Everything had to be bought and sold on the same day because refrigeration did not exist in India until recently.

The vendors were very proud of their exquisite vegetables and fruit, and encouraged the shoppers to inspect and handle the produce so that they could select the freshest and ripest. That contact is an important part of shopping for food—especially in the bazaars—so I was very disappointed when I came to America and found all the produce in supermarkets covered in cellophane, and that it was taboo to touch or smell anything. This inaccessibility dimin-

ished the whole experience of shopping and cooking. Although this practice is still normal in most markets, more and more places in the West are adopting the Eastern style of selling—allowing the shoppers to touch and squeeze and select for themselves the things they want to buy. I always shop in these places whenever I can, and I advise everyone else to do so.

There are, however, many fresh produce farms all over the countryside in America which grow and sell their own fruit and vegetables, and often jams, pickles, and freshly baked pies as well. About six miles from my house in upstate New York is Holmquest Farm, which I discovered when I moved to the area eighteen years ago, and which remains my favorite.

Like the other fresh produce farms, Holmquest has a large variety of seasonal fruit and vegetables available from April until November, but Holmquest is unique in that it is owned and run by this wonderful and photogenic old lady whose appearance puts me in mind of a benevolent beautiful witch—as opposed to a malevolent one. She must be about ninety years of age now, but in all the years I've known her she has always looked exactly the same, except for having lost one or two teeth, and her temperament is similarly constant. She is always smiling and cheerful, never grumpy or short-tempered.

Whatever you buy—peppers, tomatoes, beans, squash, anything in fact—if you are a favored customer she'll add an extra piece for good luck. Members of her family help her out in the shop, as well as the farm, but she deals with her favorite customers herself—and I can claim to be one of those. I always tell her that I have come all the way from Bombay to buy her produce, and so she adds an extra ear of corn, or tomato, or bean to my shopping basket. She's never suspected that my story is anything but the gospel truth because she invariably introduces me as her friend from Bombay.

Each year my dear friends Gwen Reed and Bruno Pasquier-Desvignes, the writer and painter, give an open-house strawberry party in May and buy what seems like twenty bushels of strawberries from Holmquest. The day after the party I go to our benevolent witch and ask her where all her strawberries have gone. She tells me they have been sold to her friends Gwen and Bruno and asks me whether I know them. This charade goes on every year like a saga—and it's difficult to know who is teasing whom.

If I call at the farm and she is not there—she sometimes visits the bowling alley in a nearby town for a game—I miss her. It's just not the same when she's not there. The vegetables are the same, of course, but buying them isn't as much fun.

Sarson-walli Asparagus

Fresh Asparagus in Mustard Dressing

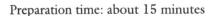

Preparation time: about 15 minutes

Serves 4

  20 asparagus spears, woody portions cut off
  2 tablespoons Dijon mustard
  2 tablespoons tarragon vinegar
  ¼ teaspoon salt
  ¼ teaspoon ground red pepper

Steam the asparagus until tender, about 10 minutes.

Meanwhile, whisk together the mustard, vinegar, salt, and red pepper.

Drain the asparagus, if necessary, and place them on a warmed serving platter. Pour the mustard sauce over the asparagus and serve.

Posho
Green Beans

❖

Preparation time: 20 minutes

Serves 4–6

    1 pound fresh green beans
    2 tablespoons vegetable oil
    1 small whole dried red chili
    ½ teaspoon ajwain (lovage) seeds
    ½ teaspoon cumin seeds
    ½ teaspoon black mustard seeds
    1 teaspoon salt, or to taste
    ½ teaspoon ground red pepper
    Pinch of turmeric

Wash the beans and trim off ends. Cut the beans into ½-inch pieces. Heat the oil in a frying pan, add the dried chili, and let it cook for 2 minutes. Add the ajwain, cumin, and mustard seeds and fry for 1 minute. Add the beans, salt, red pepper, and turmeric. Stir-fry for 5 to 10 minutes. The beans should remain crisp.

Nimbu aur Lasson-walli Broccoli

Broccoli in Garlic-Lemon Butter

Preparation time: about 15 minutes

Serves 3–4

1 pound broccoli
6 tablespoons butter
Juice of 2 medium lemons
4 garlic cloves, peeled and minced
1 teaspoon ground red pepper
1 teaspoon cumin seeds

Discard any thick, coarse ends on the broccoli and steam or cook in boiling water for 8 to 10 minutes, or until just tender. Be careful not to overcook; it should remain green and slightly crisp.

Meanwhile, melt the butter in a saucepan over low heat with the lemon juice, garlic, red pepper, and cumin seeds. Pour the garlic-lemon butter over the broccoli and serve hot.

Gobi Tamatar
Stewed Cauliflower and Tomatoes

Preparation time: 35–40 minutes

Serves 4

6 tablespoons vegetable oil
½ medium onion, peeled and chopped
1 medium cauliflower, cleaned and cut into small florets
3 bay leaves
2 medium tomatoes, chopped
¼ cup vinegar
Juice of ½ lemon
½ teaspoon salt
½ teaspoon ground red pepper

Heat the oil in a saucepan over medium-low heat. Add the onion and cook until it begins to brown.

Add the cauliflower and bay leaves, then the tomatoes, vinegar, lemon juice, salt, and red pepper. Cover and cook over low heat for 30 minutes, or until the cauliflower is tender. Remove bay leaves before serving.

Makai aur Hari Mirch
Fresh Corn with Chilies

◆

Preparation time: 20 minutes

Serves 4

6 ears of fresh corn
3 tablespoons vegetable oil
¼ teaspoon mustard seeds
1 cup milk
Salt to taste
Pinch of asafetida
2 teaspoons sugar
½ teaspoon turmeric
6 fresh hot green chilies, seeded and chopped
A small piece of fresh ginger root, chopped
1 tablespoon chopped fresh coriander leaves
Grated fresh coconut, for garnish (optional)
Juice of 1 lemon

Husk the corn and scrape the kernels off the cobs and into a large bowl.

Heat the oil in a deep pan and add the mustard seeds. When they begin to crackle, add the corn. Stir it in well and then add the milk, salt, asafetida, sugar, turmeric, chilies, and ginger.

Stir well over medium heat until the mixture becomes a thick paste, making sure it does not scorch or stick to the bottom of the pan. Remove the pan from the heat.

Transfer to a heated serving bowl and garnish with coriander leaves. If desired, sprinkle with fresh coconut. Finally, pour the lemon juice evenly over the top. Serve hot.

Tamatar Makai
Corn with Tomato and Coriander Sauce

❖

Preparation time: 20–30 minutes

Serves 10–12

4 medium tomatoes
½ bunch fresh coriander leaves and stems
3 tablespoons vegetable oil
1 whole dried red chili
2 garlic cloves, peeled and crushed
½ teaspoon black mustard seeds
½ teaspoon cumin seeds
1-inch piece of fresh ginger root, peeled and grated
1 small fresh hot green chili, split and seeded
1¼ teaspoons salt
½ teaspoon ground red pepper
Pinch of turmeric
4½ cups corn kernels (three 11-ounce cans or three 10-ounce packages frozen)

Process the tomatoes and coriander in a food processor until coarsely chopped. Heat the oil in a saucepan, add the dried chili and fry for about 1 minute. Add the garlic, mustard seeds, and cumin seeds and fry for a minute longer. Add the tomato and coriander mixture, then the ginger, green chili, salt, red pepper, and turmeric. Cook for 5 minutes, add the corn, and simmer for 5 to 7 minutes longer. Serve hot.

Ismail Merchant's Passionate Meals

Challia Dahi
Corn with Yogurt

❖

Preparation time: 10–15 minutes

Serves 4–6

2 tablespoons vegetable oil
1 dried red chili
½ teaspoon black mustard seeds
½ teaspoon cumin seeds
2 cups corn kernels (fresh, thawed frozen, or drained canned)
½-inch piece fresh ginger root, peeled and grated
¾ teaspoon salt (or to taste)
Pinch of turmeric
¼ teaspoon ground red pepper
2 tablespoons plain yogurt

Heat the oil in a skillet. Add the dried red chili and let it fry for 1 minute. Add the mustard and cumin seeds and cook for 1 minute. Add the corn, ginger, salt, turmeric, and red pepper and stir in well. Add the yogurt, cover, and simmer for 5 minutes. Serve hot.

Karhai Brinjal
Braised Eggplant

◆

Preparation time: 20 minutes

Serves 4

  ½ cup vegetable oil
  1 large onion, peeled and sliced
  3 garlic cloves, peeled and chopped
  1 large eggplant, unpeeled, cut into cubes
  2 plum tomatoes, quartered
  2 tablespoons vinegar
  4 bay leaves
  ½ teaspoon salt
  ¼ teaspoon ground red pepper

Heat the oil in a large saucepan. Add the onion and garlic and cook for 3 to 5 minutes. Add the eggplant cubes and cook for a few minutes, stirring occasionally. Stir in the tomatoes, vinegar, bay leaves, salt, red pepper, and ½ cup water and continue cooking over medium heat for about 15 minutes. Remove the bay leaves.

Baigan Bhartha

Puréed Eggplant

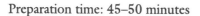

Preparation time: 45–50 minutes

Serves 8–10

2 large eggplants
¼ cup vegetable oil
1 large onion, peeled, quartered, and sliced
3 medium tomatoes, chopped
1 fresh hot green chili, split lengthwise
½ teaspoon ground red pepper
Salt to taste
1 tablespoon chopped fresh coriander leaves

Rub the eggplants lightly with oil. Place the eggplants in a preheated broiler pan and position it so that the top surfaces of the eggplants are 5 or 6 inches away from the source of heat. Turn frequently and cook for about 30 minutes, until the eggplants feel soft and the skin is charred. Peel, then mash the pulp with a fork.

Heat the oil in a saucepan. Add the mashed eggplant and stir over low heat for 3 to 5 minutes. Add the onion and cook for 5 minutes. Stir in the tomatoes, chili, and red pepper. Add salt to taste. Transfer to a warmed serving bowl and garnish with coriander.

Methi aur Bhaji Baigan

Fenugreek Leaves with Eggplant

❖

Preparation time: 15 minutes

Serves 6

1 pound fresh fenugreek leaves (or spinach leaves)
1 eggplant (about 1 pound)
2 tablespoons vegetable oil
½ teaspoon turmeric
1 teaspoon ground cumin
1 teaspoon ground coriander
1 teaspoon ground red pepper
Pinch of asafetida
Salt to taste

Remove and discard the stems from the fenugreek leaves, cut up the leaves and wash well. Cut the eggplant into 1-inch chunks. In a large skillet, heat the oil. Add the eggplant, turmeric, and seasonings. Gently squeeze out the water from the fenugreek leaves and add them to the eggplant. Cook, stirring occasionally, until the vegetables are tender.

Rai-walli Kumbhi

Mushrooms Sautéed in Mustard Oil

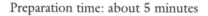

Preparation time: about 5 minutes

Serves 3–4

> 3 tablespoons mustard oil (see Note)
> ¼ cup lemon juice
> 4 bay leaves
> 1 teaspoon ground red pepper
> 12 medium mushrooms, sliced

Heat the oil in a saucepan over low heat. Add the lemon juice, bay leaves, and red pepper, and cook for 1 minute.

Stir in the mushrooms and cook for 3 to 4 minutes. Be careful not to overcook. Remove bay leaves before serving.

NOTE: Mustard oil, the oil extracted from mustard seeds, is sold in Indian grocery stores. If it's not available, you can substitute light vegetable oil.

Bhindi
Sautéed Okra

◆

Preparation time: 15–20 minutes

Serves 4–6

    1 pound okra
    2 tablespoons vegetable oil
    1 teaspoon cumin seeds
    1 large onion, peeled and sliced fine
    1 fresh hot green chili, seeded and chopped
    1 large tomato, chopped fine
    1½ teaspoons salt
    ½ teaspoon ground red pepper
    Pinch of turmeric
    Chopped fresh coriander to garnish

Wipe the okra pods with a damp cloth. Do not wash them, as this will make them sticky. Cut off and discard the ends. Slice the pods into ½-inch pieces.

Heat the oil in a large skillet, add the cumin, and cook for a few minutes, until lightly toasted. Put in the okra and stir frequently until lightly browned. Add the onion and green chili and cook for 5 to 7 minutes, stirring well. Put in the tomato, salt, red pepper, and turmeric and stir until well blended and heated through. The onion should still be crisp. Garnish with chopped coriander.

Ismail Merchant's Passionate Meals

Hare Muttar ki Curry
Green Pea Curry

❖

Preparation time: 15 minutes

Serves 6

2 tablespoons vegetable oil
Pinch of baking soda
½ teaspoon salt
Pinch of asafetida
4 fresh hot green chilies, ground to a paste
½-inch piece of fresh ginger root, peeled and ground to a paste
2 pounds fresh green peas (2 cups shelled)
Chopped fresh coriander leaves, to garnish
Grated fresh coconut, to garnish

Combine the oil, baking soda, salt, asafetida, ground chilies, and ginger with 2 cups of water in a pan. Stir well and place on the fire. When hot, put in the green peas. These will cook in 10 minutes. The peas should not change their color.

Remove the pan from the heat and serve, garnished with the coriander and coconut.

Matar Paneer
Green Peas with Cheese

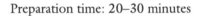

Preparation time: 20–30 minutes

Serves 6–8

3 tablespoons vegetable oil
1 small onion, chopped fine
½ teaspoon cumin seeds
1 medium tomato, chopped fine (or ½ cup canned tomato)
1-inch piece fresh ginger root, peeled and grated
1 teaspoon salt
¼ teaspoon ground red pepper
Pinch of turmeric
1 cup green peas (fresh or frozen)
Paneer from 4 cups of milk (page 76)
Fresh coriander leaves, for garnish

Heat the oil in a skillet and cook the onion until golden brown. Add the cumin seeds and fry for 2 to 3 minutes. Add the tomato and ginger, salt, red pepper, and turmeric. Cook for 3 to 4 minutes, until well blended. Add the peas. (If using frozen peas, add the paneer immediately. If using fresh peas, cook them, covered, for 5 minutes before adding the paneer.) Cover and cook gently for 8 to 10 minutes. Serve garnished with coriander.

Ismail Merchant's Passionate Meals

Tali Simla Mirch
Sautéed Bell Peppers

Preparation time: 20 minutes

Serves 4

2 large bell peppers
3 tablespoons plus 1 teaspoon vegetable oil
¼ teaspoon mustard seeds
Pinch of asafetida
2 teaspoons besan (chick-pea flour)
1 teaspoon sugar
Salt, ground red pepper, and turmeric to taste
Juice of ½ lemon

Wash the bell peppers, remove the seeds, and cut into thin long strips.

Heat 3 tablespoons of oil and the mustard seeds in a pan. When they begin to crackle, add the asafetida and peppers. Sauté, covered, until tender, about 10 minutes.

Meanwhile, mix together the besan, sugar, salt, red pepper, turmeric, and 1 teaspoon of oil. When the peppers are tender, sprinkle this mixture over them. Do not stir. Cover for 3 minutes. Lower the heat (to avoid splattering), uncover, increase the heat, and stir. When dry, remove from the heat and sprinkle the mixture with lemon juice.

Palak Bharta
Merchant's Spinach Purée

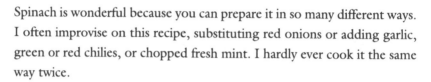

Spinach is wonderful because you can prepare it in so many different ways. I often improvise on this recipe, substituting red onions or adding garlic, green or red chilies, or chopped fresh mint. I hardly ever cook it the same way twice.

Preparation time: 10 minutes

Serves 2

  1½ pounds fresh spinach, washed and trimmed, OR 1 (10-ounce) package frozen spinach, thawed
  2 scallions
  1 tablespoon butter
  1 tablespoon Dijon mustard
  ½ teaspoon salt

Put the fresh spinach in a large pan of boiling water and cook, stirring occasionally, until tender, about 1 to 3 minutes. If frozen spinach is used, heat it following package directions.

Drain the spinach through a colander, pressing the greens with the back of a spoon to get rid of the excess moisture.

Place the spinach, scallions, butter, mustard, and salt in a food processor. Purée the mixture and serve hot.

Palak Paneer

Spinach with Cheese

❖

Preparation time: 15–20 minutes

Serves 6–8

1½ pounds of fresh spinach
Paneer from 4 cups of milk (see page 76)
Vegetable oil for deep frying
6 tablespoons butter
1 small onion, peeled and finely chopped
½ teaspoon cumin seeds
2 garlic cloves, peeled and crushed
1-inch piece fresh ginger root, peeled and grated
¼ teaspoon ground red pepper
½ teaspoon ground black pepper
1 teaspoon salt (or to taste)
Pinch of turmeric

Wash the spinach well. Cook it in a saucepan with ½ cup of water for 2 or 3 minutes. When tender, drain and chop.

Cut the paneer into 1-inch cubes. Heat 2 inches of oil to 375°F in a deep heavy pan. Fry the cubes of paneer in batches, turning over once or twice, until they are light brown. Remove the paneer with a slotted spoon. Drain on paper towels.

In a large skillet, melt the butter with 1 tablespoon of oil over medium heat and cook the onion until just beginning to turn brown. Add the cumin seeds and garlic and cook for 2 minutes. Add the ginger,

spinach, red and black pepper, salt, and turmeric, and stir well. Add the paneer and simmer, covered, for 10 minutes. Serve hot.

Paneer
Homemade Cheese

❖

Paneer is used in a variety of Indian dishes. This is the basic recipe. In most Indian homes a muslin cloth is used for draining out the excess water, but you can use a sieve.

Preparation time: 10 minutes, plus cooling

Serves 6

4 cups milk

3 tablespoons yogurt OR 1 tablespoon vinegar OR the juice of 1 lemon

Heat the milk in a saucepan, stirring, until it boils. Add the yogurt, vinegar, or lemon juice, and stir over medium heat until the mixture curdles. This takes about 2 or 3 minutes. If it doesn't curdle, add a little more yogurt, vinegar, or lemon juice.

Remove the pan from the heat and drain the mixture through a sieve. Press down gently with a spoon to make a flat, solid mass of cheese. The sieve should preferably have a flat bottom. Leave the cheese to cool for 2 hours. It should be fairly solid, but you should be able to cut it.

Jeera Paneer

Paneer with Cumin

◆

Preparation time: 10–15 minutes

Serves 4

3 tablespoons vegetable oil
½ teaspoon plain cumin seeds
Paneer from 4 cups milk (see opposite page)
½ teaspoon roasted and crushed cumin seeds
¼ teaspoon ground red pepper
½ teaspoon ground black pepper
½ teaspoon salt
Juice of ½ lemon

Heat the oil in a frying pan. Add the plain cumin seeds and cook for 2 or 3 minutes. Cut the paneer into 2-inch pieces and add to the pan. Sprinkle with the roasted cumin seeds, red and black pepper, salt, and lemon juice. Cook, turning the paneer occasionally, for 5 to 7 minutes, or until the paneer is golden brown and the spices are well blended. Serve immediately.

Shalgam
Turnips with Ginger

Preparation time: 30 minutes

Serves 4–6

    2 tablespoons vegetable oil
    1 small onion, peeled and chopped fine
    ½ teaspoon cumin seeds
    1 medium tomato, chopped fine
    1-inch piece fresh ginger root, peeled and grated
    1 teaspoon salt
    ¼ teaspoon ground red pepper
    ¼ teaspoon ground black pepper
    1½ pounds white turnips, peeled and sliced

Heat the oil in a saucepan and cook the onion until lightly browned. Add the cumin and fry for 1 minute. Add the tomato, ginger, salt, and red and black pepper. Stir and cook for 2 or 3 minutes. Add the turnips and ½ cup water and stir well. Cover the saucepan and simmer for 15 to 20 minutes. The turnips should be mushy. If they're not, mash them with a wooden spoon.

Teekhi Tarkari
Zucchini with Whole Green Peppercorns

❖

Preparation time: 15 minutes

Serves 4–6

2 tablespoons olive oil
4 medium zucchini, trimmed and sliced into rounds
1 fresh hot green chili, seeded and chopped
2 garlic cloves, peeled and sliced
1 tablespoon whole green peppercorns
1 teaspoon ground black pepper
¼ teaspoon salt
Juice of ½ lemon

Heat the oil in a large skillet and add the zucchini slices. Reduce the heat, add the green chili and garlic, and stir. Add the peppercorns, pepper, salt, and lemon juice, and sauté on a low flame for 10 minutes. Then cover the pan and cook 2 minutes more. I like vegetables crisp, but if you prefer them tender you can cook the mixture a little longer.

Zeers Mukhon-walli Gilki
Grilled Zucchini with Cumin Butter

❖

Preparation time: 10 minutes

Serves 6

6 medium zucchini

FOR THE CUMIN BUTTER:

1½ teaspoons ground red pepper
3 tablespoons butter, softened
¼ teaspoon salt
4 to 6 garlic cloves, peeled and finely chopped
1 teaspoon ground cumin

Preheat the broiler. Slice the zucchini into halves lengthwise.

Stir the cumin butter ingredients together in a bowl and spread over the zucchini slices.

Arrange the zucchini in a flameproof serving dish and grill 4 to 5 inches from the source of heat for about 8 minutes, or until just tender. Serve hot.

Dhokle

Coconut Dumplings in Vegetable Stew

This is a dish that belongs very much to my family, and I can remember it from my earliest childhood. It was prepared at least once a month, and there would often be a request from the family for it. When I came to know Jennifer Kendal (sister of Felicity Kendal) and Shashi Kapoor the actor, and they began to dine at our house, they asked for it too. Later on, this dish became known as "Jennifer's dumplings," and whenever Jennifer telephoned and my mother heard her voice she would say, "I'm making Jennifer's dumplings for you."

Preparation time: 1½ hours plus overnight soaking

Serves 6

½ cup kabli chana (white chick-peas), picked over and washed
½ cup kala chana (brown chick-peas), picked over and washed

FOR THE GREEN SPICE PASTE:

6 to 8 fresh hot green chilies, seeded if desired
2 garlic cloves, peeled and chopped
1-inch piece fresh ginger root, peeled and grated
1 tablespoon cumin seeds

FOR THE DUMPLINGS:

½ large fresh coconut
1 cup besan (chick-pea flour)
1 cup millet flour
½ cup rice flour

3 tablespoons vegetable oil

2 tablespoons ghee or clarified butter, melted

2 teaspoons ground coriander

½ teaspoon turmeric

About 1 teaspoon ground red pepper

FOR THE VEGETABLE STEW:

¼ to ½ cup vegetable oil

1 onion, chopped

6 bay leaves

¼ pound cauliflower, cut into small florets

¼ pound green beans, trimmed

¼ pound shelled green peas

¼ pound green or red bell pepper, seeded and chopped

½ pound tomatoes, chopped

3 cups hot water

½ pound potatoes, cut in large cubes

¼ pound eggplant, cut in large cubes

Salt to taste

Plain boiled rice

Soak the kabli chana and kala chana in cold water overnight. Drain.

Next make the green spice paste. Put the chilies, garlic, ginger, and cumin into a mortar or strong bowl and pound with a pestle to make a smooth paste, or process them in a food processor or blender.

To prepare the coconut for the dumplings: Pierce the eyes with a skewer and drain off the liquid. Place the coconut in a 400°F oven for 25 minutes, or until the shell cracks. Break the coconut into pieces with a hammer and when cool, separate the white meat from the shell. Remove the brown inner skin, grate the coconut with a hand grater, or put the coconut pieces in a food processor or blender and process to make fine crumbs.

To make the dumplings, mix together the besan, millet flour, and rice flour in a bowl. Add the oil and ghee. Add a quarter of the green spice paste, the coriander, turmeric, red pepper, and three-quarters of the coconut. Stir to make a fairly firm dough, adding a little water if necessary. Form the dough into small, fist-shaped dumplings.

To make the stew, heat the oil in a large saucepan and fry the onion and bay leaves over medium heat for 5 to 10 minutes, until the onion is light brown, stirring occasionally. Add the cauliflower, green beans, peas, peppers, and drained chick-peas, and cook for 15 minutes, stirring occasionally. Stir in the remaining green spice paste and the tomatoes; continue cooking for 5 minutes. Add the hot water and bring to a boil. Add the dumplings, potatoes, eggplant, and remaining grated coconut. Season with salt and simmer, partially covered, over low heat for 30 to 40 minutes, or until the chick-peas are tender. Remove bay leaves and serve with plain boiled rice.

K a r d h i

"Curry"

Kardhi, pronounced "curri," is the dish that gave the English language the word "curry"—the blanket term that in most people's perception describes Indian food. The dish is best when made with the fresh leaves of the curry plant, which is native to India and as yet unavailable in this country, but dried leaves can be purchased in Indian grocery stores.

Preparation time: 20–30 minutes

Serves 6

2 cups plain yogurt
1½ tablespoons besan (chick-pea flour)
2 fresh hot green chilies, seeded and puréed in a blender
A small piece of fresh ginger root, peeled and finely chopped
2 teaspoons sugar
Salt to taste
2 tablespoons ghee or butter
1 teaspoon mustard seeds
1 teaspoon fenugreek seeds
A stalk of curry leaves
A pinch of asafetida

Put the yogurt and besan in a large pot, add 12 cups of water, and whisk to blend. Add the green chilies, ginger, sugar, and salt. Bring to a boil and cook for 20 minutes, then remove from the heat. The kardhi is ready.

In a small skillet, heat the ghee or butter and add the mustard seeds and fenugreek seeds. When they begin to crackle add the curry leaves and asafetida. Remove the pan from the heat and pour the mixture into the kardhi. Serve hot. This should be eaten with boiled rice or kicheri (page 139).

POTATOES—
an Essential Element

Potatoes are universal throughout India and, like lentils and bread, part of daily consumption. The potato is one of the cheapest and most adaptable of vegetables, and in India we have hundreds of varieties of potato dishes. One can do without meat and fish and poultry, but the potato is as essential an element to an Indian meal as wine is to a French meal.

Just as the pommes frites made in France taste different and better than anywhere else in the world, so I find the Indian potato dishes I make in England and America never taste quite the same as they do in India. I think there must be something about the climate or the atmosphere in India that really adds something to the aloo (potato) dishes there. Nevertheless, they taste good no matter where they are prepared.

Normally aloo and pooris (a deep-fried puffy bread which is eaten hot) are made at home, because most Indians love cooking and eating at home, although restaurant culture is very much a part of metropolitan life. But street vendors trading in aloos and pooris are a common sight in Indian cities, especially in the north, and their cry of "Aloo-poori" brings people running. Similarly, all except the very grandest sweetmeat sellers, the halwais, sell aloo and pooris.

In India we describe a very round person as looking like a potato, gowl matool, and it's taken as a sort of compliment.

Aloo aur Hari Piyaz ki Sabzi

Boiled Potatoes with Scallions and Chives

❖

Preparation time: 15–20 minutes

Serves 4

    1½ pounds small potatoes
    6 tablespoons snipped chives
    3 scallions, chopped
    4 garlic cloves, peeled and chopped
    4 tablespoons (½ stick) butter
    2 fresh sage leaves, chopped
    ½ fresh hot green chili, seeded (optional) and chopped
    Salt to taste

Cook the unpeeled potatoes in boiling water for 15–20 minutes, or until they are just tender; drain and cut each one into 2 or 3 pieces.

While the potatoes are still hot, gently toss with the chives, scallions, garlic, butter, sage, chili, and salt to taste. Serve hot.

Ismail Merchant's Passionate Meals

Aftari Aloo
Fasting Day Potatoes

◆

This is a celebratory dish I created after a day of fasting.

Preparation time: about 20 minutes

Serves 3–4

4 medium potatoes
3 tablespoons vegetable oil
1 medium onion, peeled and diced
¼ cup lemon juice
1 bunch of fresh dill, stems discarded, chopped
3 garlic cloves, peeled and chopped
12 black peppercorns
½ teaspoon cumin seeds
A pinch of salt

Peel and slice the potatoes.

Heat the oil in a frying pan over medium-low heat. When hot, add the onion and cook until it begins to brown, stirring occasionally.

Stir in the potatoes and add the lemon juice, dill, garlic, peppercorns, cumin, and salt. Cook, covered, for about 15 minutes, stirring occasionally, until the potatoes are tender. Serve hot.

Aloo Tikki
Stuffed Potato Patties

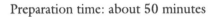

Preparation time: about 50 minutes

Serves 4

FOR THE PEA STUFFING:

> 8 ounces green peas, defrosted if frozen
> ½ teaspoon minced fresh hot green chili
> 2 tablespoons chopped fresh parsley

FOR THE SPINACH STUFFING:

> 8 ounces spinach, washed and trimmed, OR 3 ounces frozen spinach, defrosted
> 1 or 2 fresh hot green chilies, seeded (optional) and chopped
> A pinch of salt
> ¼ teaspoon ground black pepper

FOR THE POTATO PATTIES:

> 4 large potatoes, scrubbed
> 3 tablespoons vegetable oil
> 1 teaspoon ground red pepper
> ¼ teaspoon salt
> 2 tablespoons cream
> 3 large eggs, lightly beaten
> About 4 tablespoons (½ stick) butter

For the pea stuffing, cook the peas in boiling water until done and drain through a colander. Stir in the chili and parsley.

For the spinach stuffing, cook the spinach in boiling water until done, drain in a colander, and squeeze dry. Stir in the chilies, salt, and pepper.

To make the patties, cook the unpeeled potatoes in boiling water until very tender. When they are cool enough to handle, peel and then mash them very well with 1 tablespoon of the oil, the salt, red pepper, cream, and enough of the beaten eggs to make a smooth but not too soft texture. With your hands, make 8 round patties about 3 inches in diameter and ¼ inch thick. Put about a tablespoon of either filling in the center of each patty, gather up the edges, and bring them together to enclose the fillings completely. Press to seal, turn over and press down to flatten slightly.

Heat the remaining oil and the butter in a frying pan and fry the patties about 5 minutes, until lightly browned, turning once. Serve hot.

Aloo Chaat

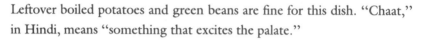

Potato Chaat

◆

Leftover boiled potatoes and green beans are fine for this dish. "Chaat," in Hindi, means "something that excites the palate."

Preparation time: about 10 minutes

Serves 4

3 tablespoons butter
1 pound potatoes, boiled, peeled, and diced
A pinch of salt
1 tablespoon of Dijon mustard
¼ pound green beans, cooked
1 tablespoon chopped fresh parsley

Melt the butter in a frying pan over medium-low heat. Add the potatoes, salt, mustard, and beans, and stir.

Cook the mixture for about 10 minutes, or until it is thoroughly hot. Sprinkle with parsley and serve immediately.

Khas Aloo
Va-Va-Voom Potatoes

One of the things I particularly like about potatoes is that you can cook more than you need for a particular meal and so have lots of leftover potatoes that can have many incarnations—like this deliciously simple recipe—over the next day, and the next, and possibly even the day after. This is why this dish is called va-va, which means "encore."

Preparation time: about 30 minutes

Serves 6

> 2½ pounds small red potatoes, scrubbed
> ½ cup tarragon vinegar
> ¼ cup walnut oil
> 8 dried red chilies, seeded if desired
> 1½ teaspoons dill weed
> 1 teaspoon mustard seeds
> 1 teaspoon salt

Cook the unpeeled potatoes for 15–20 minutes, or until they are tender, but slightly firm. Do not overcook them.

Combine the vinegar, oil, chilies, dill weed, mustard seeds, and salt in a saucepan.

Drain and halve the unpeeled potatoes, stir them into the vinegar and oil mixture, and cook for 10 minutes, covered, over low heat. Serve hot.

Masaledar Gobi Aloo
Spicy Stewed Cauliflower and Potatoes

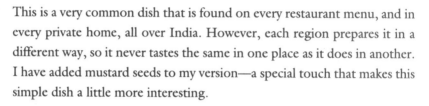

This is a very common dish that is found on every restaurant menu, and in every private home, all over India. However, each region prepares it in a different way, so it never tastes the same in one place as it does in another. I have added mustard seeds to my version—a special touch that makes this simple dish a little more interesting.

Preparation time: 45–50 minutes

Serves 4–6

¼ cup vegetable oil
1 medium onion, peeled and chopped
2 large potatoes, peeled and cut into small pieces
1 teaspoon ground red pepper
¼ cup lemon juice
1 teaspoon salt
¼ teaspoon turmeric
1 medium cauliflower, washed and cut into florets
1 fresh hot green chili, seeded (optional) and sliced
1 dried red chili, seeded (optional) and crushed
½ cup plain yogurt, mixed with ¼ cup of water
1 teaspoon mustard seeds

Heat the oil in a large saucepan over medium-low heat. Add the onion and cook until it begins to turn brown, stirring occasionally.

Stir in the potatoes and cook until they also begin to brown, stirring frequently.

Add the red pepper, lemon juice, salt, and turmeric. Cook over medium-low heat for 2 to 3 minutes, stirring occasionally.

Add the cauliflower, green and red chilies, and the yogurt-water mixture, and stir well.

Continue cooking for 20 to 30 minutes, or until the vegetables are tender.

Put about 1 teaspoon of mustard seeds over the dish at the end as a garnish.

Shazeera-walla Piyaz aur Aloo ka Salaad
Caraway-Onion Potato Salad

❖

Preparation time: 30 minutes, plus chilling

Serves 8–10

5 pounds small potatoes, scrubbed
1 large onion, peeled and diced
4 garlic cloves, peeled and finely chopped
¼ cup caraway seeds
¼ cup chopped fresh parsley
Juice of 2 lemons
¼ cup Dijon mustard
¼ cup vegetable oil
5 dried red chilies, seeded (optional) and coarsely chopped
½ teaspoon salt

Cook the unpeeled potatoes in boiling water until they are just tender.

Meanwhile, in a large bowl, mix together the onion, garlic, caraway seeds, parsley, lemon juice, mustard, oil, chilies, and salt.

Refresh the potatoes under cold running water for 2 or 3 minutes, drain well, and cut in half lengthwise.

Stir the potatoes into the onion mixture and refrigerate, covered, until ready to serve.

Peela Aloo
Yellow Spiced Potatoes

This dish is particularly good served with hot, freshly made pooris (a kind of bread), when it is sometimes referred to as the "poor man's dish." In fact, the meal is suitable for a prince, particularly if accompanied by a sweet chutney, such as peach or mango.

Preparation time: 35 minutes

Serves 4–6

6 to 8 medium potatoes, peeled
½ cup vegetable oil
2 garlic cloves, peeled and chopped
½ teaspoon turmeric
½ teaspoon salt, or to taste
¼ teaspoon ground red pepper
¼ teaspoon ground cumin seeds
¼ teaspoon mustard seeds

Cook the potatoes in boiling water until they are just cooked through. Do not overcook. When cooled, cut into bite-size pieces and place in a saucepot.

In a small skillet, heat the oil and add the garlic, turmeric, salt, red pepper, ground cumin, and mustard seeds. Stir over low heat until the garlic has browned, about 3 or 4 minutes.

Pour the mixture over the top of the potatoes and stir gently to combine. Cook over medium heat for a few minutes, until they are quite hot, and serve.

Jeera Aloo
Potatoes with Cumin

Preparation time: 20 minutes

Serves 4–6

3 tablespoons vegetable oil
1 dried red chili
1 teaspoon cumin seeds
½ teaspoon black mustard seeds
4 medium potatoes, peeled and sliced
1 tablespoon plain yogurt
1 teaspoon salt
¼ teaspoon ground red pepper
¼ teaspoon turmeric

Heat the oil in a frying pan, add the whole dried chili, and cook for 2 minutes. Add the cumin and mustard seeds. When they start to sputter (about 2 minutes), add the potatoes, yogurt, salt, red pepper, and turmeric. Give it a good stir. Cover and cook over low heat until the potatoes are tender (about 15 minutes).

PULSES—
the Universal Food

In India, if you are invited to lunch or dinner and you are not served dal (lentil stew), the meal is considered incomplete. Pulses (lentils, dried beans, peas) of any sort or dal of any kind accompanies every meal—guests expect it, and the host knows it has to be provided.

Dal is the universal food of India, and every day over eight hundred million Indians eat it—with Indian breads, like roti, chapati, or nan, as a thick soup over rice; with vegetables, or simply on its own. It is common to the rich man's table and the poor man's, the only difference being the degree of sophistication or inventiveness in the way it is cooked. Most households in India take great pride in cooking a particular kind of dal dish, and often there is a family recipe that has been handed down over many generations.

Dal may appear to be a very simple food in Western terms, but in India it is the focus of the meal. I know that

European and American visitors who come to India for the first time and who have never eaten dal before are amazed to discover what can be done with the simple lentil. Dal is to India what pasta is to Italy, and the variations of dal dishes are just as extensive. I am very inventive with dal, and my lemon dal (Nimbu Masoor Dal, page 102), particularly, has become very famous. People have written about it, they talk about it, and friends travel halfway across the world to eat it with us in New York.

I can't live without dal, and if I were to be told that I could not have dal each day with my meals I would feel deprived of something essential to my eating habits. I can do without everything else including meat, fish, vegetables, rice, and bread—but I am a dal junkie, and I must have dal. If I have an attack of gout—which is rare—the doctors immediately tell me to stop eating dal, as it is full of protein and contributes to the problem. But that would be torture. So, of course, I don't stop eating dal. I'd rather take the medicine, the injections, the whole system-flushing routine—but stop eating dal? No.

Hara Masoor ki Dal

Green Lentil Dal

Preparation time: about 45 minutes

Serves 4–6

  2 tablespoons vegetable oil
  1 medium onion, peeled and chopped
  12 whole cloves
  ½ cinnamon stick, broken into pieces
  1 pound (2 cups) continental masoor (see Glossary), picked over and
    washed
  1¾ cups canned beef broth
  1½ teaspoons salt
  Juice and grated zest of 1½ medium lemons
  ½ teaspoon ground red pepper

Heat the oil in a saucepan over medium-low heat. When hot, add the onion and cook, stirring occasionally, until it begins to brown. Stir in the cloves and broken cinnamon stick and cook for 1 minute.

Add the lentils and cook for 5 minutes, stirring occasionally.

Add the broth, 3 cups of hot water, and the salt. Stir the mixture well, cover, and let it boil gently for 15 minutes over medium heat. Add the lemon juice, then toss in the zest and add the red pepper. Cook, covered, for another 15 minutes, or until the lentils are tender.

Nimbu Masoor Dal
Lemon Lentils

◆

This is one of my favorite recipes, and it was printed in *The New York Times Magazine* of March 7, 1979. It's also a favorite of many people I've cooked for, and has become a staple of my repertoire. I don't recall how it first happened. Probably by finding a lemon in the refrigerator and flinging it into a pot of cooking dal in a pretty carefree way. I always, however, associate it with the actress Felicity Kendal, for whom I first made it.

I regard Felicity as my first pupil. She had come to England right after *Shakespeare Wallah*, in which she starred, to make a life for herself, rather as the young girl Lizzie did in that film. She found a flat in Swan Court, Chelsea, with a tiny kitchen, and I gave her her first lesson in Indian cooking. Our menu was simple: tandoori chicken, pea pillau, raita, and lemon dal. Felicity helped me peel the onions, cut up the ginger, and tried not to get in my way too much. She watched very carefully as she must have watched her English relatives and friends, because in a very short time she was turning out delicious and quite complicated meals in that tiny kitchen, both Indian-style and traditional English ones. She is a natural-born cook, just as she is a natural-born actress; perhaps it is because one needs a sense of innate timing to be successful in both endeavors, cooking and acting.

Preparation time: about 1½ hours

Serves 10–12

  1¼ cups vegetable oil, divided
  2 medium onions, peeled, halved, and sliced thin
  4 (2-inch) pieces of cinnamon stick

2 pounds masoor dal (see Glossary), picked over and washed (4 cups)

1 tablespoon peeled and chopped fresh ginger root

5 cups chicken stock

Salt to taste

1 teaspoon ground red pepper

1 lemon

1 small onion, peeled and chopped

1 garlic clove, peeled and chopped

1 fresh hot green chili, chopped, with seeds

4 bay leaves

2 tablespoons chopped fresh coriander leaves

Heat ¾ cup of the oil in a large, deep saucepan over medium-low heat. When hot, add the sliced onions and cook, stirring, until they soften.

Add the cinnamon, lentils, and ginger to the pan and cook, stirring often, for about 10 minutes.

Add the stock, 4 cups of hot water, salt, and red pepper. Bring to a boil, reduce the heat, and simmer for about 10 minutes.

Squeeze the juice from the lemon. Discard the seeds. Add the lemon juice and squeezed shell and cook for about 50 minutes longer, stirring often.

Heat the remaining ½ cup of oil in a small pan. Add the chopped onion, garlic, chili, and bay leaves. Cook, stirring, until the onion is browned.

Add this mixture, including the oil, to the lentils. Remove the bay leaves. Sprinkle with the chopped coriander. Serve hot.

Kabli Chana
Chick-Pea Dal

◆

Preparation time: 2–3 hours, plus overnight soaking

Serves 6–8

> 6 cups kabli chana (beige chick-peas) OR kala chana (brown chick-peas) (see Glossary)
> 1 cup vegetable oil
> 1 teaspoon ground red pepper
> ¼ teaspoon turmeric
> 1 teaspoon caraway seeds
> 1 teaspoon salt
> 6 garlic cloves, peeled and chopped
> 1 tablespoon tamarind paste
> 4 fresh hot green chilies, seeded if desired
> 1 tablespoon chopped parsley

Soak the chick-peas overnight in plenty of cold water. Drain well.

Heat the oil in a saucepan over medium heat. When hot, add the red pepper, turmeric, and caraway seeds, and cook for 2 or 3 minutes.

Add the drained chick-peas, stir, and cook for 3 to 5 minutes more, stirring occasionally.

Add the salt, garlic, and the tamarind paste mixed in ½ cup of water. Then add 1¼ cups of hot water and the chilies. Cover tightly and cook over a low heat for 2 to 3 hours, or until the chick-peas are tender, adding more water if necessary. Sprinkle with the parsley before serving.

Amiri Khaman
Imperial Lentils

❖

Preparation time: 45–50 minutes, plus soaking

Serves 6

1 pound (2 cups) chana dal (yellow split peas)
1 cup vegetable oil
1 teaspoon mustard seeds
A pinch of asafetida
10 or 12 fresh hot green chilies, ground in a blender
A small piece of gingerroot, peeled and chopped
15 garlic cloves, peeled and chopped
½ teaspoon turmeric
Salt to taste
2 teaspoons sugar
Juice of ¼ lemon
1 cup milk
2 tablespoons chopped fresh coriander leaves
¼ fresh coconut, meat removed and grated
Store-bought sev (chick-pea-flour noodles)

Soak the chana dal in water for 6 to 8 hours. Drain and grind coarsely in a food processor or with a mortar and pestle, forming a thick paste. If necessary, add a little water, but use as little as possible.

Heat the oil in a large saucepan and add the mustard seeds. When they begin to crackle, add the asafetida and the dal paste, stirring constantly to prevent sticking.

When the mixture is dry, add the green chilies, ginger, garlic, turmeric, salt, sugar, and lemon juice; stir well. Sprinkle in 2 tablespoons of milk every 5 minutes, and keep stirring over medium-low heat. Repeat until all the milk has been added and is absorbed.

When the dal separates from the pan, the khaman is ready. Spread it on a thali, or large flat plate, and garnish with the coriander and coconut. Top with fine ready-made salted sev.

Mag-ki Chhuti Dal
Green Gram Mustard Dal

❖

Preparation time: 35 minutes, plus soaking

Serves 2–4

4 ounces moong dal (split mung beans)
1 tablespoon vegetable oil
¼ teaspoon mustard seeds
¼ teaspoon asafetida
¼ teaspoon turmeric
½ teaspoon ground red pepper
Salt to taste
1 tablespoon chopped fresh coriander leaves

Soak the moong dal in water for 4 hours. Heat the oil in a saucepan, add the mustard seeds and, when they begin to crackle, add the asafetida and 1 cup of water. Next, add the turmeric, red pepper, and salt. Bring the water to a boil.

Drain the dal and add it to the boiling water. Cook, partially covered, for about 30 minutes. When tender, remove from the heat and transfer to a warmed serving bowl. Each grain of dal should be separate. Garnish with the coriander. Serve hot.

Sherbanu's Masoor Dal
Sherbanu's Red Lentil Dal

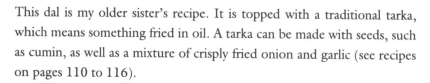

This dal is my older sister's recipe. It is topped with a traditional tarka, which means something fried in oil. A tarka can be made with seeds, such as cumin, as well as a mixture of crisply fried onion and garlic (see recipes on pages 110 to 116).

Preparation time: 45 minutes

Serves 6–8

2 cups masoor dal (red lentils), picked over and rinsed
1 tablespoon peeled and chopped fresh ginger root
¼ teaspoon turmeric
1 teaspoon salt
1 teaspoon ground red pepper
1 tomato, quartered
¼ cup vegetable oil
1 small onion, sliced thin
2 garlic cloves, chopped fine

Combine the dal, ginger, turmeric, and 6 cups of water in a pot and boil for 15 to 20 minutes.

Add the salt, red pepper, and tomato. Cook for another 10 minutes and transfer to a serving dish.

Heat the oil in a large skillet and sauté the onion and garlic until tender (making the tarka). Pour the tarka onto the center of the cooked dal just before serving.

Ma Dal
Whole Black Beans

Preparation time: 3½ hours, plus soaking

Serves 6–8

½ cup ma dal (whole urid, or dried black beans, see Glossary)
1 small handful red kidney beans
1-inch piece of fresh ginger root, peeled and grated
½ cup canned tomatoes, chopped small
2 whole cloves
1 cinnamon stick
1 teaspoon salt
1 small dried red chili
8 tablespoons (1 stick) butter
1 cup milk
Tarka (see page 110)
Fresh coriander to garnish

Pick the dal over carefully and remove any foreign objects. Wash it 4 or 5 times in cold running water. Soak the dal and the kidney beans in water overnight to soften.

Combine the beans with the ginger, tomatoes, cloves, cinnamon, salt, and whole dried chili in a pressure cooker with about 6 cups of water. Cook under pressure for 20 to 30 minutes. Remove the lid and add the butter and milk. Simmer, covered loosely, for 2½ or 3 hours, stirring occasionally. Garnish with tarka and fresh coriander.

Tarka with Cumin

See Sherbanu's Masoor Dal on page 108 for an onion-garlic version of this traditional fried garnish.

Preparation time: 5 minutes

½ onion, chopped fine
4 tablespoons (½ stick) butter
1 tablespoon vegetable oil
1 teaspoon cumin seeds
½ teaspoon ground red pepper

Brown the onion in a small pan with the butter and oil. Add the cumin and red pepper. Stir, but not too much, and pour over dal.

Chahar Dal
Mixed Dal

Preparation time: 50 minutes

Serves 6–8

  1 tablespoon chana dal (yellow split peas)
  1 tablespoon split masoor dal (red lentils)
  2 tablespoons moong dal (split mung beans)
  2 tablespoons toor dal (split yellow lentils, see Glossary)
  1 medium tomato, chopped
  2 or 3 curry leaves (optional)
  Juice of 1 lemon
  1 teaspoon salt
  1-inch piece fresh ginger root, peeled and grated
  Onion-Garlic Tarka (see below)

Wash all the dals. Put in a saucepan with the tomato, curry leaves, lemon juice, salt, and grated ginger. Add 4 cups of water and bring to the boil. Cover and simmer for 40 or 45 minutes, until the mixture is thick and souplike. Garnish with tarka.

Onion-Garlic Tarka

Preparation time: 5 minutes

3 tablespoons vegetable oil
1 small onion, sliced thin
3 garlic cloves, peeled and crushed, or chopped fine
½ teaspoon ground red pepper
¼ teaspoon turmeric
Fresh coriander leaves, for garnish

Heat the oil in a small skillet and brown the onion. Add the garlic, red pepper, and turmeric and cook for 2 minutes, then tip it into the dal mixture. Mix in lightly. Garnish with the coriander.

Moong Bean Pot
Moong Dal

❖

Preparation time: 25 minutes

Serves 4–6

    1 cup moong dal, washed and picked over
    1 small tomato, chopped fine
    1-inch piece fresh ginger root, peeled and grated
    1 small fresh hot green chili
    1 teaspoon salt
    Garlic Cumin Tarka (see page 114)

Place the dal in a large saucepan. Add 3 cups of water, the tomato, ginger, chili, and salt and bring to a boil. Cover and simmer for 15 to 20 minutes, until the dal mixture is well blended and has the consistency of a soup. Garnish with tarka.

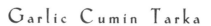

Garlic Cumin Tarka

Preparation time: 5 minutes

2 tablespoons vegetable oil
2 garlic cloves, peeled and crushed
½ teaspoon cumin seeds
¼ teaspoon ground red pepper
¼ teaspoon ground black pepper
Fresh coriander leaves, for garnish

Heat the oil in a small frying pan, and add the garlic and cumin seeds. Fry for 2 minutes. Add the red and black pepper and immediately pour over the dal. Garnish with the coriander.

Toor Dal
Toor Bean Pot

◆

Preparation time: 45 minutes

Serves 8–10

6 ounces toor dal (split pigeon peas), picked over

1-inch piece of fresh ginger root, peeled and grated

1 fresh hot green chili, split

1 tomato, chopped

1 to 2 teaspoons salt

½ teaspoon tamarind (imli) essence OR 2 to 3 tablespoons soaked
    strained tamarind OR the juice of 3 lemons

3 to 4 teaspoons sugar (for a "sweet and sour" taste)

6 dried curry leaves

Mustard Seed Tarka (see below)

Wash the dal 2 or 3 times in cold water and put into a pressure cooker
with 5 cups of water. Add the ginger, chili, tomato, and salt. Put on the
pressure and cook for 5 minutes with the pressure up. Turn off the heat.
When the pressure is down remove the lid. Add the tamarind essence, the
sugar, and the curry leaves. Taste and add more tamarind or sugar as
required. Cook, uncovered, over low heat until well blended. Garnish
with tarka.

Mustard Seed Tarka

Preparation time: 5 minutes

> 2 tablespoons vegetable oil
> ¾ teaspoon black mustard seeds
> ¼ teaspoon ground red pepper
> 2 dried red chilies (remove seeds if you prefer it less hot)

Heat the oil, then add the mustard seeds, red pepper, and chilies. When the mustard seeds pop, pour immediately over the dal. Stir lightly.

Raj Ma
Red Kidney Beans

◆

Preparation time: 1 hour 20 minutes, plus soaking

Serves 6–8

3 tablespoons vegetable oil

1 medium onion, chopped fine

½ teaspoon cumin seeds

3 medium tomatoes, finely chopped

½-inch piece fresh ginger root, peeled and grated

1½ teaspoons salt

¼ teaspoon ground red pepper

Pinch of turmeric

1 fresh hot green chili, split

1 cup red kidney beans (soaked overnight)

1 tablespoon plain yogurt

Fresh coriander leaves, for garnish

Heat the oil in a pressure cooker and fry the onion until golden brown. Add the cumin seeds and cook for 2 minutes. Add the tomatoes, ginger, salt, red pepper, turmeric, and the split green chili and cook for 5 minutes.

Drain the kidney beans and add to the pan. Add the yogurt and cook for a further 5 minutes. Add 4 cups of water and cook under pressure for 15 to 20 minutes. When the pressure is down, remove the lid and simmer gently for about 30 to 45 minutes, until the ingredients are well blended. Garnish with coriander.

Bhindi Dal
Okra Dal

❖

Preparation time: 40 minutes

Serves 6–8

   ½ cup olive oil
   1 medium onion, peeled and sliced
   1 teaspoon cumin seeds
   2 cinnamon sticks, broken up
   2 cups masoor dal (red lentils), picked over and rinsed
   1 teaspoon ground coriander
   ½ teaspoon ground red pepper
   ¼ teaspoon turmeric
   1 large tomato, halved
   ½ teaspoon salt
   20 whole okras, ends nipped off

Heat the oil in a deep pot. Cook the onion with the cumin seeds and cinnamon sticks over medium heat until the onion begins to brown.

Add the dal, ground coriander, red pepper, and turmeric, and stir. Cook for 2 minutes.

Add 5 cups of water. Stir and bring to a boil. Add the tomato, salt, and okras. Cover and cook for 20 to 25 minutes.

Kale Chana/Chole
Whole Black Chick-Peas

Preparation time: 40 minutes, plus soaking

Serves 6–8

  1 cup black chick-peas, picked over and soaked overnight
  2 teaspoons salt
  2 tablespoons vegetable oil
  1 dried red chili
  ½ teaspoon black mustard seeds
  ½ teaspoon cumin seeds
  3 garlic cloves, crushed
  ¼ teaspoon turmeric
  Juice of ½ lemon
  Ground red pepper to taste
  Handful of fresh coriander leaves for garnish

Boil the chick-peas in a pressure cooker in about 4 cups of water with 1 teaspoon of salt. After about 20 minutes they should be tender. Drain.

In a large skillet, heat the oil, add the whole red chili, and fry it for about 2 minutes. Add the mustard seeds, cumin seeds, and garlic, and cook for about 2 minutes. Add the chick-peas, 1 teaspoon of salt, turmeric, lemon juice, and red pepper. Stir, cover, and let it simmer for about 15 minutes. Garnish with coriander.

Aloo Chole
Potatoes and Chick-Peas

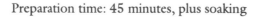

Preparation time: 45 minutes, plus soaking

Serves 6–8

TO MAKE THE CHICK-PEAS:

  8 ounces white chick-peas (soaked overnight in cold water)
  A pinch of baking soda
  1 heaping tablespoon chana dal (yellow split peas)
  2 whole black cardamom pods
  3 whole cloves
  10 peppercorns
  1 teaspoon salt

TO MAKE THE SAUCE:

  3 medium potatoes, peeled
  3 tablespoons vegetable oil
  1 medium onion, quartered and sliced
  1 teaspoon ground cumin
  3 medium tomatoes, finely chopped
  2-inch piece of fresh ginger root, peeled and grated
  ½ teaspoon salt, or to taste
  ½ teaspoon ground red pepper
  1 fresh hot green chili, split
  Pinch of turmeric
  Juice of 2 lemons

Ismail Merchant's Passionate Meals

$\mathcal{C}$ombine the chick-peas, baking soda, chana dal, cardamom pods, cloves, peppercorns, and salt in a pressure cooker with 4 cups of water and cook under pressure for 15 minutes. (Or cook in a saucepan for 1½ to 2 hours or until tender, adding water as needed.) Remove the pan from the heat.

To make the sauce, cook the potatoes in boiling water until tender. Meanwhile, heat the oil in a large saucepan and cook the onion until lightly browned. Add the cumin and let it sizzle for a few minutes. Add the tomatoes and ginger and turn down the heat. Add the salt, red pepper, green chili, and turmeric, and cook for 3 to 5 minutes, until well blended. Stir the lemon juice into the sauce. Taste to check whether it needs more salt or lemon. Cut the potatoes into eighths. Add the chick-peas with their liquid and the potatoes to the sauce, stir, and cook for a further 20 to 30 minutes, until well blended.

Serve this with bhaturas (see page 264).

Besan Walla Chana
Black Chick-Peas with Gram Flour Sauce

❖

Preparation time: 45 minutes, plus soaking

Serves 6–8

  1 cup black chick-peas, picked over and soaked overnight
  2 teaspoons salt
  3 tablespoons vegetable oil
  1 small dried red chili
  ½ teaspoon cumin seeds
  ½ teaspoon black mustard seeds
  2 garlic cloves, peeled and crushed
  1-inch piece ginger root, peeled and grated
  2 medium tomatoes, finely chopped
  Pinch of turmeric
  1 tablespoon besan (gram flour, or chick-pea flour)
  Juice of 1 lemon
  Fresh coriander leaves for garnish

Boil the chick-peas and 1 teaspoon of salt with 4 cups of water in a pressure cooker for 15 to 20 minutes or until tender. In a saucepan, heat the oil, add the dried chili, and fry it for about 2 minutes. Add the cumin seeds, mustard seeds, and garlic and cook for 2 minutes. Add the ginger, tomatoes, 1 teaspoon salt, and turmeric and cook until the tomatoes are well blended with the oil and spices. Add the besan and stir. Cook for another 10 minutes. Add the chick-peas and the water they were cooked in, which should be about 2 cups. Stir well, add the lemon juice, and simmer for 10 to 15 minutes until it is well blended and the sauce is thick. Garnish with coriander.

Palak, Tamatar aur Moong Dal

Spinach, Tomatoes, and Moong Dal

Preparation time: 40 minutes

Serves 4

> 1 pound fresh spinach leaves
> ½ cup moong dal (split mung beans)
> 3 tomatoes, chopped
> 1 medium onion, chopped
> Salt to taste
> ½ teaspoon ground red pepper
> A little gur (or soft, dark brown sugar)

Wash the spinach and place in a pan. Pick over and wash the dal and place on the spinach. Add ½ cup of water. Bring to a boil, cover, and cook over low heat for 30 minutes, or until the moong dal is tender. Add the tomatoes, onion, salt, red pepper, and gur. Cook for 3 minutes. Mix well, remove from the heat, and serve.

Lauki Dal
Squash with Split Chana Lentils

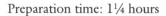

Preparation time: 1¼ hours

Serves 6–8

  1 tablespoon vegetable oil
  1 medium onion, peeled and sliced
  ½ teaspoon whole cumin seeds
  2 medium tomatoes, chopped
  1-inch piece of fresh ginger root, grated
  ¼ teaspoon ground red pepper
  1 teaspoon salt, or more, to taste
  ¼ teaspoon turmeric
  ½ pound lauki (also known as ghiya or kiya, similar to a small marrow squash but with a harder texture) or other squash
  1 cup chana dal (yellow split peas)
  Handful of fresh coriander leaves for garnish

Heat the oil in a saucepan and sauté the onion until brown. Add the cumin seeds and cook for 2 or 3 minutes, until the seeds start sputtering. Add the tomatoes, ginger root, red pepper, salt, and turmeric and cook for about 5 to 7 minutes over low heat.

While that is cooking, peel the lauki and cut into 1-inch pieces. Wash the dal. Add the lauki to the tomato-onion mixture and cook for 10 to 15 minutes. Add the dal and 1 cup of water. Cover the saucepan and simmer for about 45 minutes, until the dal is well blended and cooked through. Garnish with coriander.

EACH GRAIN ...
SEPARATE
AND FULL OF
FLAVOR

Rice is a staple food throughout India, but particularly in South India and Bengal. Like dal, rice accompanies almost every meal.

Back home, people boasted that each grain of my grandmother's rice was separate and full of flavor. Many Westerners complain that they can never get their rice to come out right, that it is soggy or too sticky. There is a special art to cooking rice, but I challenge anyone who follows my method not to produce perfect results. My rule of thumb when cooking rice is to fill the saucepan with one half inch of water above the level of the rice. If you do this your rice will never fail. It will always be absolutely perfect, and the enjoyment of eating it will be much greater because it has been so little trouble to cook.

A word or two of caution, however: Rice burns fast if you turn your back for a minute and go off to make a telephone call, as I am afraid I do all too often. To avoid a scorched taste, then, watch it carefully. Turn the heat down to the lowest possible level for the last five minutes of cooking.

Before cooking, I like to rinse basmati rice in several changes of water until the water runs clear. I then tip it into a bowl, cover it with plenty of fresh cold water, and leave it to soak for thirty minutes. Then I tip the rice and water into a sieve and leave it to drain for another ten minutes before cooking it. I feel this gives it a superior texture and appearance. But if you are short of time, you can just rinse it once and leave out the soaking. I nearly always use the latter method, as I never give myself enough time.

There are many varieties of rice available, and it's best to try out small quantities of each type until you find the one you prefer. However, never buy instant rice, which is dreadful. I often use standard packaged long-grain rice, which is universally available, but my first choice is always basmati rice, which can be found in Indian groceries and in many health-food stores.

Basmati is a special long-grain rice from India and Pakistan and it has a unique flavor and aroma. It should be picked over, as it sometimes contains small stones and twigs,

and then washed in several changes of water. This rinses off the excess starch that causes the grains to stick together. Basmati rice is then soaked in more fresh water for thirty minutes and drained, and this cuts down the amount of water used in cooking. The result is worth taking this trouble.

Sabzi Pullao
Vegetable Pilaf

Preparation time: 40 minutes

Serves 6

    2 medium onions, peeled and chopped
    6 black cardamom pods
    ½ cup vegetable oil
    1 teaspoon ground red pepper
    1 teaspoon salt
    1 teaspoon garam masala (see page 13)
    ¼ teaspoon turmeric
    2 tablespoons vinegar
    2½ cups water
    3 potatoes, with skins, quartered
    4 carrots, peeled and cut into 2-inch slices
    1 dozen snow peas
    1 dozen string beans, halved
    3 medium tomatoes, chopped
    2 cups uncooked basmati rice, washed

In a large saucepot, brown the onions and cardomom pods in oil over medium heat.

Make a paste of the red pepper, salt, garam masala, turmeric, and vinegar. Add this to the above mixture and cook for 5 minutes.

Add 2½ cups of water to the mixture. When the water comes to a boil, add the potatoes, parboiled beforehand if desired, the carrots, snow peas, string beans, and tomatoes, and cook for about 10 minutes.

Add the rice, stir, and cover. Cook for an additional 15 minutes.

Zafrani Pullao
Saffron Pilaf

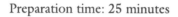

Preparation time: 25 minutes

Serves 4

2 tablespoons butter

1 cinnamon stick

1¼ cups chicken stock

½ teaspoon salt

4 bay leaves

2 cups uncooked rice

8 strands of saffron

5 ounces slivered almonds

Melt the butter in a large saucepan with the cinnamon stick. Add the stock, salt, bay leaves, and 2 cups of water and bring the liquid to a boil.

Add the rice, cover, and cook over very low heat for 10 minutes.

Add the saffron, and cook for another 10 minutes, or until the rice is tender, stirring occasionally. Remove bay leaves.

Sprinkle with the almonds and serve.

EACH GRAIN ... SEPARATE AND FULL OF FLAVOR

Basmati Pullao
Basmati Pilaf

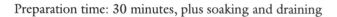

Preparation time: 30 minutes, plus soaking and draining

Serves 4

  1½ cups uncooked basmati rice, picked over
  2 tablespoons vegetable oil
  1 medium onion, peeled and chopped
  2-inch piece of cinnamon stick
  2 whole cloves
  1 bay leaf
  4 ounces cashews
  2 ounces sultanas (golden raisins)
  1 teaspoon salt

Wash the rice in several changes of cold water until the water is clear; cover it with plenty of more cold water and leave it to soak for 30 minutes.

Let the rice drain through a sieve for about 30 minutes.

Heat the oil in a large skillet over medium-low heat and cook the onion until it is soft.

Add the drained rice, cinnamon stick, cloves, bay leaf, cashews, and sultanas, and stir-fry the mixture for 2 minutes over medium heat.

Add 2 cups of water to the pan with the salt and bring to a boil. Cover tightly. Turn the heat to low and simmer for 20 minutes, adding a little extra water during cooking if necessary, until the rice is tender and fluffy, and all the water is absorbed.

Remove bay leaf and cinnamon stick before serving.

Peela Chaaval
Yellow Turmeric Rice

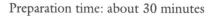

Preparation time: about 30 minutes

Serves 8

- 2 tablespoons butter
- 1 medium onion, peeled and chopped
- 4 black cardamom pods
- 2½ cups chicken stock
- 2 teaspoons cumin seeds
- 2 cups uncooked long-grain white rice
- ¼ teaspoon turmeric

Melt the butter in a large saucepan over medium-low heat. Add the onion and cook, stirring occasionally, until the onion begins to brown.

Add the cardamom pods and cook for 1 to 2 minutes, stirring occasionally.

Add the stock and 2¼ cups of water. Bring to a boil; add the cumin seeds, rice, and turmeric.

Cook, covered, over low heat for 20 minutes, or until the rice is tender, stirring occasionally.

Tej Pati Chaaval
Brown Rice with Bay Leaves

❖

Preparation time: about 50 minutes

Serves 4–6

    4 tablespoons (½ stick) butter
    3 or 4 bay leaves
    1 teaspoon salt
    1¾ cups uncooked brown rice

Melt the butter in a large saucepan over low heat with the bay leaves.

Add 2½ cups of water and the salt to the pan and bring the liquid to a boil.

Add the rice, cover tightly, and turn the heat to low. Cook for 45 minutes, or until the rice is just tender.

Mattar Pullao
Green Pea Pilaf

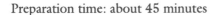

Preparation time: about 45 minutes

Serves 8–10

  1 cup vegetable oil
  3 medium onions, peeled and chopped
  2 cinnamon sticks, broken up
  1-inch piece of fresh ginger root, peeled and chopped
  1 teaspoon ground red pepper
  ¼ teaspoon turmeric
  1 teaspoon cumin seeds
  3½ cups uncooked long-grain white rice
  2 cups green peas, defrosted if frozen
  4 tablespoons (½ stick) butter

Heat the oil in a large saucepan over medium-low heat. When hot, add 2 of the chopped onions, the cinnamon sticks, ginger, red pepper, turmeric, and cumin seeds. Cook for 10 minutes, stirring occasionally.

Carefully add 2 cups of water and bring to a boil. Add the rice, lower the heat, cover, and simmer for 15 minutes, or until the rice is fluffy.

Add the peas, stir well, cover, and cook for a further 10 minutes.

Meanwhile, melt the butter in a pan over medium heat. Add the remaining chopped onion and cook, stirring frequently, until the onion is brown and crisp.

Spread the hot onion and butter over the top of the pilaf to serve.

Kotmir Illaichi-wale Chaaval
Cardamom and Coriander Rice

◈

Preparation time: about 45 minutes

Serves 6–8

 2 tablespoons butter

 2¼ cups uncooked long-grain white rice

 4 black cardamom pods

 ½ teaspoon ground red pepper

 ½ teaspoon salt

 3 tablespoons finely chopped fresh coriander leaves OR parsley leaves

Melt the butter in a large saucepan over medium-low heat. Add the rice, cardamom pods, and red pepper and cook for 6 or 7 minutes, stirring constantly. Watch carefully so the rice does not stick or burn.

Stir in 3¼ cups of water and the salt. Bring the water to a boil, then cover the pan tightly and cook over very low heat for about 20 minutes, or until the rice is just tender.

Remove the pan from the heat and let the rice rest, covered, for 5 to 10 minutes.

Transfer to a warmed serving dish, sprinkle the chopped coriander leaves over the rice, and serve.

Brinjal Pullao
Eggplant Pilaf

Preparation time: 35 minutes

Serves 4

2 cups uncooked basmati rice

1 medium eggplant

4 tablespoons (½ stick) butter

4 fresh hot green chilies, chopped

A small piece of fresh ginger root, crushed

½ teaspoon cumin seeds

2 teaspoons poppy seeds or couscous

¼ cup peanuts, roasted and coarsely ground

1 tablespoon sugar

Salt to taste

Wash and drain the rice and set aside. Peel the eggplant and cut into small pieces.

Heat the butter in a large saucepan and add the chilies, ginger, cumin seeds, poppy seeds, and peanuts. When the mixture is slightly brown, add the sugar and cook until it turns dark brown. Add the eggplant and salt. Stir briskly.

Put in 4 cups of hot water, raise the heat, and when it simmers add the rice. Stir gently. Cover and cook on low heat until the rice is done, about 20 minutes. Remove the pan from the heat and serve hot.

Sherbanu Pullao
Sherbanu's Rice

This recipe comes from my older sister, Sherbanu.

Preparation time: 25 minutes

Serves 10–12

    3 tablespoons butter
    24 black peppercorns
    1 tablespoon cumin seeds
    1 teaspoon salt
    6 cups uncooked basmati rice, washed until the rinse water is clear

In a large heavy pot, combine the butter, peppercorns, cumin seeds, and salt. Add 8 cups of water. Bring to a boil.

Add the rice, stir, and cover. Cook over medium heat for about 20 minutes, or until all the water has been absorbed and the rice is tender.

Sherbanu Kicheri
Sherbanu's Lentils and Rice

◈

My sister Sherbanu, who is a wonderful cook, was visiting us in New York and decided she would prepare her favorite kicheri for us. We invited a few people to dinner that night, and they all loved her kicheri so much that this rice and lentil dish disappeared in five minutes—and they barely touched the rest of the food.

Preparation time: 30 minutes

Serves 4–6

3 tablespoons corn oil
1 small onion, sliced
2 garlic cloves, sliced
2 bay leaves
1¾ cups uncooked basmati rice, washed until the rinse water is clear
¼ cup masoor dal (red lentils), picked over and washed
1 tablespoon salt
1 cinnamon stick, broken up

In a deep saucepan over medium heat, heat the oil. Cook the onion, garlic, and bay leaves until the onion is lightly browned.

Mix the rice and dal and add it to the above mixture. Add the salt, the cinnamon stick, and 1½ cups of water. The water should cover the mixture by about ½ inch if the pot is the right size. Bring to a boil, stir, then cover.

Cook about 12 to 15 minutes. Do not stir to the bottom to discover if it is cooked. You can tell if it is done when little funnel-shaped holes appear on the top of the kicheri and it no longer looks very moist. It should be steaming a bit.

Jeera Rice
Basmati Rice with Cumin

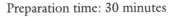

Preparation time: 30 minutes

Serves 6

    1½ cups uncooked basmati rice
    3 tablespoons vegetable oil
    ½ teaspoon cumin seeds
    2 (2-inch) lengths of cinnamon stick
    4 whole cloves
    1¼ teaspoons salt

Wash the rice in 3 changes of cold water, then soak for 15 to 20 minutes in fresh cold water. Heat the oil in a saucepan and when hot add the cumin, cinnamon, and cloves. Cook for 5 minutes, then add the rice, salt, and 2½ cups of water. Cover and bring to a boil. Stir once. Turn the heat down to low and simmer gently, covered, for 10 to 12 minutes, or until all the water is absorbed.

Biryani
Rice with Spiced Meat

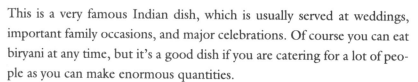

This is a very famous Indian dish, which is usually served at weddings, important family occasions, and major celebrations. Of course you can eat biryani at any time, but it's a good dish if you are catering for a lot of people as you can make enormous quantities.

In my film *In Custody,* there is a scene (which became known as the "biryani scene") in which the poet Nur and his disciples eat biryani and drink a good deal of rum and get very drunk. My editor on the film, Roberto Silvi, who had watched this scene repeatedly and had heard us talk endlessly about biryani, finally demanded, "What *is* this biryani?" So Shahrukh Husain, who wrote the Urdu script for the film, and had come to New York for a few days, offered to make it for us. Coincidentally, the biryani was appropriate that evening for we had a number of reasons to celebrate—the last day of editing, Ruth and Cyrus Jhabvala's forty-second wedding anniversary, and a surprise visit from Om Puri. Om, one of the actors in my film, had stopped off in New York for a few days on his way back to India from Los Angeles, where he had been making a film with Jack Nicholson. Shahrukh cooked a wonderful biryani and, unlike the film, it wasn't accompanied with rum. We had a very fine Haut-Brion and, as it was a celebration, some even finer Champagne.

Preparation time: 1½ hours

Serves 14

> 2 large cardamom pods (black or green)
> 6 cloves
> ½ teaspoon ground cinnamon, OR ½-inch cinnamon stick

½ teaspoon cumin seeds

¼ cup plus 2 tablespoons vegetable oil or ghee

6 medium onions, thinly sliced

6 pounds of chicken parts, skinned and cut up into 3-inch pieces

1 medium garlic clove

½-inch piece fresh ginger root

1 teaspoon ground red pepper

1 teaspoon cumin powder

1 generous teaspoon turmeric

2 large or 3 medium fresh whole green chilies

16 ounces plain yogurt

2 pounds basmati rice

6 medium potatoes, boiled, quartered, and deep-fried

1 cup tomato juice

1 teaspoon saffron powder (optional)

1 cup milk (optional)

In a mortar and pestle, pound together the cardamom, cloves, cinnamon, and cumin seeds. Place ¼ cup of vegetable oil in a large heavy-based pot. Add the pounded spices and half the onions and fry, stirring, until the onions take on a good brownish-gold color. Add the chicken pieces and fry for 2 minutes.

Meanwhile, grind the garlic, ginger, red pepper, cumin powder, and turmeric into a paste. Add to the onions, along with the whole green chilies. When the fragrance of the spices starts to rise, add half the yogurt and stir briskly. Cover the pot and tenderize over very low heat for about 20 minutes, checking frequently. If the meat starts falling off the bone, that's OK. Add water if needed; the liquid should be on a level with the top of the meat without covering it, and should have the consistency of a thick sauce.

Boil the rice, making sure it is not entirely cooked but slightly under-boiled. Drain the water completely from the rice and leave in a colander.

Take a fresh pot. Put in the remaining 2 tablespoons of oil and cover

with a generous layer of cooked rice. Add a layer of chicken, the potatoes, and the remaining onions, then the tomato juice, the remaining yogurt, and the rest of the rice. If using the saffron, dilute the saffron powder in a cup of milk and add over the top of the rice. Cover the pan with a clean tea towel and place the lid firmly on the tea towel to seal the pan completely. Leave on a very low heat for 20 to 30 minutes.

Serve with raita and an onion and tomato salad.

CHEERING UP CHICKEN

The poultry eaten most in India is chicken, although sometimes duck and wild fowl are served. Chicken, like beef, has a special status in Indian kitchens, and is served to dinner guests and on special occasions.

There was no refrigeration in India when I was a boy, so the chickens were brought to the market alive and slaughtered only when they had been sold. They were always fresh and very tender and tasty.

Unfortunately, I have never been able to recapture the same taste with the prepackaged frozen—or even the fresh—chickens available in the West, where chicken is considered almost a convenience food and doesn't seem to taste of anything. I try to cheer it up with some interesting and flavorful sauces.

However, it's been exciting to discover the possibilities of the much wider variety of poultry here. Every year we

celebrate Thanksgiving with the traditional turkey—but
never with a traditional stuffing. Since I've been celebrating
Thanksgiving, which has now become a very important meal
to me, I must have used every possible combination of
Indian ingredients for the stuffing—including leftover dal.
And I doubt that I've ever stuffed our turkey the same
way twice.

Shazeera-walla Murgh Mussallam
Red Pepper—Caraway Roast Chicken

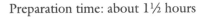

Preparation time: about 1½ hours

Serves 4

1 whole chicken, about 3½ pounds
1 lemon, cut in half
½ teaspoon salt
½ to 1 teaspoon ground red pepper
1 teaspoon caraway seeds

Heat the oven to 375°F. Squeeze the lemon halves over the chicken and place the rinds in the chicken cavity (or fill the cavity with stuffing—see recipes that follow). Sprinkle with salt and red pepper, then with caraway seeds.

Place the bird in a greased baking pan and roast for 1½ hours, or until tender.

Serve with Lemon Lentils (page 102) and Raw Spinach Salad (page 52).

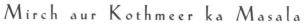

Mirch aur Kothmeer ka Masala
Chili and Parsley Stuffing for Poultry

Preparation time: 5 minutes

Enough for a 3½-pound chicken

½ cup plain yogurt
2 dried red chilies, seeded if desired and finely chopped
¼ teaspoon ground red pepper
¼ teaspoon salt
3 tablespoons chopped fresh parsley
1¼ cups dry bread crumbs

Mix together all the ingredients.

Chilla aur Chutni-walla Murgh
Pancake and Chutney Stuffing for Chicken

Preparation time: 5 minutes

Enough for a 3½-pound chicken

2 tablespoons spicy-hot chutney
1-inch piece of fresh ginger root, peeled and grated
1 fresh hot green chili, seeded (if desired) and chopped
5 tablespoons vinegar
1 teaspoon salt
1 cup fresh, cold pancakes torn into small pieces

Combine all the ingredients and mix thoroughly.

Nimboo Adrak aur Mirch ka Murgh Mussallam

Lemon, Ginger, and Chili Stuffing for Chicken

Preparation time: 5–10 minutes

Enough for a 3½-pound chicken

2 fresh hot green chilies, seeded if desired and coarsely chopped
1 lemon, seeded and chopped
2-inch piece of fresh ginger root, peeled and chopped
¼ teaspoon salt
½ teaspoon ground black pepper
1¼ cups dry bread crumbs
1 teaspoon caraway seeds

Combine the chilies, lemon, ginger, salt, and pepper in a blender or food processor and process until finely chopped. Or chop them together well using a knife.

Blend the bread crumbs and caraway seeds into the lemon mixture.

Rai Murgh Muhammar

Roast Chicken with Parsley and Mustard

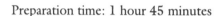

Preparation time: 1 hour 45 minutes

Serves 4

FOR THE STUFFING:

> 3 tablespoons olive oil
> 2 tablespoons mustard
> 3 garlic cloves, chopped
> 2 dozen pistachios, shelled
> 3 slices whole-grain bread, cut into chunks
>
> 1 whole chicken (about 3½ pounds)
> 2 tablespoons Dijon mustard
> 2 tablespoons olive oil
> Juice of ½ lemon
> Salt to taste
> Ground red pepper to taste
> Dried parsley flakes

Preheat the oven to 375°F.

Make the stuffing: Mix the olive oil, mustard, and garlic together thoroughly, add the pistachios, and toss with the bread chunks. Stuff loosely into the chicken.

Mix together the mustard, olive oil, lemon juice, salt, and red pepper and pour over the chicken. Cover the chicken with parsley flakes and roast for 1½ hours, or until tender.

Tej Sahed Wali Murg

Hot and Honey—Roasted Chicken

Preparation time: 1½ hours

Serves 6

FOR THE STUFFING:

> ½ loaf of good Italian bread, cubed (about 3 cups)
> 1 large onion, peeled and sliced
> 1 tomato, chopped
> 15 green beans, steamed and cut into 2-inch lengths
> 3 fresh hot green chilies, seeded and chopped
>
> 1 roasting chicken, about 5 pounds
> Salt and pepper to taste
> 2½ ounces Hot and Honey condiment (see Note)
> Olive oil

Mix all the stuffing ingredients together and fill the chicken loosely. Sprinkle salt and pepper all over the chicken. Rub the Hot and Honey condiment over the chicken, then drizzle with olive oil. Roast in a 375°F oven for 1½ to 2 hours, or until the chicken is cooked through.

NOTE: This can be purchased in some specialty food shops, or you can make something similar by adding ground red pepper to honey.

Dahi Murgh I
Yogurt Chicken I

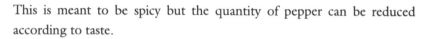

This is meant to be spicy but the quantity of pepper can be reduced according to taste.

Preparation time: 1 hour 20 minutes

Serves 10–12

½ cup vegetable oil
2 medium onions, peeled and chopped
4 dried whole red chilies
12 whole cloves
5½ pounds chicken drumsticks and thighs
1-inch piece fresh ginger root, peeled and grated
1½ cups plain yogurt
1 teaspoon salt
1 tablespoon ground black pepper

Heat the oil in a large heavy-based frying pan or saucepan over medium heat. When hot, add the onions, chilies, and cloves, and cook, stirring frequently, until the onions brown.

Add the chicken and ginger and stir continually until the meat is seared on all sides.

Mix the yogurt with 1 cup of water and add to the pan with the salt and pepper. Cover and cook over medium-low heat, stirring occasionally, for 1 hour. Serve with rice and a green salad.

*J*umbo
Shrimp in
Lemon and
Ajwain

Lamb Pullao
with Cucumber
Raita

*P*icking ripe vegetables from my garden at the Big House, Upstate New York

Selecting fresh corn cobs – no matter how many or how few I buy, the benevolent "beautiful witch" who owns the farm will always throw in an extra one for luck.

The "beautiful witch" of Holmquest Farm. In the eighteen years I've known her and shopped at her farm she hasn't changed at all – except for losing one or two teeth.

*F*resh sweet
corn, squash,
peppers and
artichokes

$\mathcal{L}$obsters,
coconut and
garlic

Finished dish, garnished with whole mushrooms and fresh basil leaves

 $\mathcal{A}$ variety
of beans and
pulses

𝒷asmati Pilaf,
Chicken with Parsley
and Mustard Sauce,
garnished with whole
mushrooms.

*V*eal with
mustard and
dill sauce,
Zucchini with
Whole Green
Peppercorns

The dining room
at the Big House,
Upstate New York –
the table is laid
for dinner

*D*inner at the Big House, Upstate New York. Clockwise from the head of the table: the author, Linda Dosio, Joe Dosio, Jatinder Chohan, James Ivory, Rizwan Chowhan, Cyrus Jhabvala (obscured), Ruth Prawer Jhabvala (obscured)

Dahi Murgh II
Yogurt Chicken II

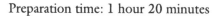

Preparation time: 1 hour 20 minutes

Serves 10–12

½ cup vegetable oil
2 medium onions, peeled and chopped
1 bay leaf
5½ pounds chicken drumsticks and thighs
2 teaspoons cumin seeds
1½ cups plain yogurt
1½ teaspoons ground red pepper
1 teaspoon salt
1 large tomato, quartered

Heat the oil in a large heavy-based frying pan or saucepan over medium heat. When hot, add the onions and bay leaf. Cook, stirring frequently, until the onions brown.

Add the chicken and cumin seeds and stir continually until the meat is seared on all sides.

Blend the yogurt and ½ cup of water together and add to the pan with the red pepper and salt.

Add the quartered tomato, cover, and cook over medium heat, stirring occasionally, for 1 hour. Remove bay leaf before serving. Serve with Basmati Pilaf (page 132) and Pistachio Raita (page 18).

Tamatar Murgh
Tomato Chicken

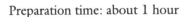

Preparation time: about 1 hour

Serves 6

- ½ cup vegetable oil
- 1 large onion, peeled and chopped
- 1 cinnamon stick, broken into pieces
- 4 black cardamom pods
- 1 chicken, about 3 pounds, cut through the bones into about 10 small pieces
- 2 teaspoons caraway seeds
- 2 teaspoons ground black pepper
- ½ teaspoon salt
- 4 large tomatoes, sliced
- 1 bunch fresh parsley, chopped

Heat the oil in a skillet over medium heat. When hot add the onion, cinnamon, and cardamom pods. Cook, stirring frequently, until the onion is brown, about 5 minutes.

Add the chicken, caraway seeds, pepper, and salt, and cook, covered, over medium-low heat for 15 minutes. Stir every few minutes.

Add the tomatoes and chopped parsley, turn the heat to low, and cook, stirring occasionally, for 30 minutes, until the chicken is tender. Serve with Basmati Pilaf (page 132).

Kali Mirch Murgh

Pepper Chicken

❖

Preparation time: 1–1¼ hours

Serves 4

½ cup vegetable oil
2 medium onions, chopped
7 black cardamom pods
1 teaspoon cumin seeds
1 chicken, about 3 pounds, cut into serving pieces
Juice of 2 medium lemons
2 tablespoons ground black pepper
2 tablespoons green peppercorn mustard
½ teaspoon salt
6 garlic cloves, peeled and crushed

Heat the oil in a large heavy-based saucepan over medium heat. When hot, add the onions, cardamom pods, and cumin seeds and cook, stirring frequently, until the onions begin to brown.

Add the chicken pieces and cook, stirring frequently, for 10 minutes.

Mix the lemon juice, black pepper, mustard, and salt with 1 cup water, and pour the mixture over the chicken and onions. Let the mixture cook, covered, over medium-low heat for 15 minutes.

Add the garlic and continue cooking for 30 to 40 minutes, stirring occasionally, until the meat is tender; add a little more liquid if necessary to prevent burning. Serve with Basmati Pilaf (page 132) and Cucumber Raita (page 16).

Murgh Masala
Spicy Chicken Curry

While we were shooting *Quartet* in Paris, Maggie Smith succumbed to my Spicy Chicken Curry, served with Spicy Stewed Cauliflower and Potatoes (see page 94). Later I prepared my Mackerel in Coconut Sauce (see page 222) for her during the shooting of *A Room with a View*.

Preparation time: 45 minutes

Serves 4

3 tablespoons vegetable oil

1 large onion, sliced

6 peppercorns

1 cinnamon stick

4 cardamom pods

6 whole cloves

2 bay leaves, crumbled

1 chicken, about 3 pounds, cut into serving pieces

¼ teaspoon turmeric

½ teaspoon ground red pepper

½ teaspoon ground coriander

½ teaspoon ground cumin

½ teaspoon ground ginger

Salt to taste

2 garlic cloves, peeled and crushed

½ cup plain yogurt

½ teaspoon ground allspice

$\mathcal{H}$eat the oil in a large saucepan over medium heat. When hot, add the onion, peppercorns, cinnamon, cardamom pods, cloves, and bay leaves. Cook, stirring frequently, until the onion turns light brown.

Add the chicken pieces and cook, stirring frequently, until the meat is seared on all sides.

Sprinkle in the turmeric, red pepper, coriander, cumin, ginger, and salt to taste. Stir in the garlic. Continue cooking, stirring occasionally, until the chicken is well colored.

Add 1¾ cups of hot water, cover, and simmer about 30 minutes, or until the chicken is just cooked. Add the yogurt and allspice and simmer for another 10 minutes. Serve with Green Pea Pilaf (page 135) and Cucumber Raita (page 16).

Murgh Dam
Baked Chicken

Preparation time: 2 hours, plus marinating time

Serves 4–6

2 tablespoons vegetable oil

5 or 6 garlic cloves, peeled and crushed

3-inch piece of fresh ginger root, peeled and grated

4 teaspoons garam masala

1 teaspoon ground red pepper

2 to 3 teaspoons salt

1 cup plain yogurt

Juice of 2 lemons

1 (3-pound) chicken, skinned and cut into serving pieces

In a large skillet, heat the oil and add the garlic, ginger, garam masala, red pepper, and salt. Cook for 2 or 3 minutes. Stir in the yogurt. Remove from the heat and allow to cool. Add the lemon juice.

Wash the chicken pieces and arrange in an ovenproof casserole. Pour the yogurt marinade over the chicken, turning to coat well. It is best to let it sit in the refrigerator for 6 to 8 hours, covered.

Preheat the oven to 350°F and bake the chicken in its marinade, uncovered, for 1 to 1½ hours, or until it is tender.

Murgh Masala

Spicy Chicken

❖

Preparation time: 45–50 minutes

Serves 6–8

 3 tablespoons vegetable oil
 2 medium onions, peeled and chopped
 1 fresh hot green chili
 4 garlic cloves, peeled and crushed
 2 teaspoons garam masala
 2 teaspoons salt
 ½ teaspoon ground red pepper
 ¼ teaspoon turmeric
 4 medium tomatoes, chopped
 2-inch piece of fresh ginger root, peeled and grated
 4 pounds chicken, skinned and cut into small pieces
 ¼ cup plain yogurt

Heat the oil in a large saucepan and brown the onions and chopped chili over low heat. Add the garlic, garam masala, salt, red pepper, and turmeric and cook for 2 or 3 minutes. Add the tomatoes and ginger and stir well. Simmer for 5 to 7 minutes, until the spices are well blended. Add the chicken pieces and yogurt. Stir well, cover, and simmer for about 30 minutes, or until the chicken is tender.

If you prefer, you can bake this in the oven, first mixing the chicken with the tomato and spices and then transferring it to a covered casserole dish. Bake it at 400°F for 30 minutes, or until the chicken is cooked through.

Murgh Duncan
Chicken Duncan

Preparation time: 2½ hours

Serves 4–6

    1 (14-ounce) can tomato purée
    4 to 6 fresh tomatoes
    1 cup plain yogurt
    Juice of 2 lemons
    ½ bunch fresh coriander
    ½ teaspoon ajwain seeds
    2 to 3 teaspoons salt
    5 garlic cloves, peeled
    2-inch piece of fresh ginger root, peeled
    2 teaspoons garam masala
    1 fresh hot green chili, seeded and coarsely chopped
    ½ teaspoon ground red pepper
    1 chicken (about 3 pounds), skinned and cut into pieces
    8 small potatoes, peeled (optional)
    2 medium onions, peeled and quartered (optional)

In a food processor, make a marinade by blending the tomato purée, tomatoes, yogurt, lemon juice, coriander, ajwain seeds, salt, garlic, ginger root, garam masala, green chili, and red pepper. (You may have to do this in batches.)

    Wash and dry the chicken pieces and place them in a large ovenproof casserole. Add the marinade and stir together well. Let the chicken marinate in the refrigerator for about an hour.

If you are using potatoes and onions, add them to the casserole, stirring to coat them with the marinade. Arrange the chicken pieces and vegetables in one layer. Cover the casserole and bake in a preheated 350°F oven for about 1½ hours or until the chicken is very tender.

Dhaniya Mursh
Coriander Chicken

◆

Preparation time: 45 minutes

Serves 4–6

- 4 tablespoons (½ stick) butter
- 1 tablespoon vegetable oil
- 4 large garlic cloves, peeled and crushed
- 2-inch piece of fresh ginger root, peeled and grated
- 2 to 3 teaspoons salt
- 1 teaspoon ground red pepper
- ¼ teaspoon turmeric
- 1 tablespoon garam masala
- 1 chicken (about 3 pounds), skinned and cut into serving pieces
- 1 bunch of coriander, washed and chopped
- 2 tablespoons plain yogurt

Melt the butter in a saucepan over medium heat. Add the oil and garlic, ginger, salt, red pepper, turmeric, and garam masala. Stir and cook for 2 to 3 minutes.

Add the chicken and fry lightly for 5 to 7 minutes. Add the coriander and yogurt and stir well. Cover the pan and simmer for 30 minutes, or until the chicken is cooked through.

Murgh Jeera
Chicken with Cumin

This recipe can also be used to make hors d'oeuvres. Use boneless chicken breasts cut into bite-size pieces, or use winglets or drumsticks.

Preparation time: 50 minutes

Serves 4–6

¼ cup vegetable oil
2 teaspoons cumin seeds
1 teaspoon cumin seeds, roasted and crushed
1 chicken (about 3 pounds), skinned and cut into serving pieces
2½ teaspoons salt
½ teaspoon ground red pepper
1 teaspoon ground black pepper
Juice of 2 lemons
¼ teaspoon turmeric
2 teaspoons garam masala

Heat the oil in a heavy pot and add both kinds of cumin seeds. Let them sizzle for a few minutes, then add the chicken, salt, red pepper, black pepper, lemon juice, turmeric, and garam masala. Stir to coat the chicken with the spices. Cover and cook over medium heat for 25 to 30 minutes, or until the chicken is cooked through. This can also be cooked in a covered baking dish in the oven at 350°F for about 45 minutes.

Tandoori Murgh Dan
Dan's Tandoori Chicken

❖

I made this dish for my friend Dan Rose. He is a connoisseur of great wine, and I suspected he might bring with him a spectacular bottle, so I wanted to prepare something that wouldn't overpower the wine but would match it in intensity.

Preparation time: 1½ hours

Serves 8–10

18 chicken drumsticks
¼ cup olive oil
2 dried red chilies
1 inch piece of ginger root, peeled and grated
6 small tomatoes
2 large onions, peeled and sliced
2 cups plain yogurt
8 garlic cloves, peeled and chopped
1 teaspoon ground red pepper
½ teaspoon salt

Wash and remove the skin from the drumsticks. Take a large baking sheet and cover the base with olive oil. Lay the drumsticks in the pan. Make a paste (use a food processor if you wish) with the red chilies and ginger. Cut the tomatoes in half and place in the pan. Mix the paste with the onions, yogurt, garlic, red pepper, and salt; pour over the drumsticks, coating them well. Bake uncovered in a 350°F oven for about 45 to 60 minutes.

Murgh Italvi Khas Roberto Silvi

Roberto Silvi's Cacciatore Chicken

———————————◆———————————

I was fortunate to have the distinguished Italian film editor Roberto Silvi to edit my film *In Custody*. Not only is Roberto a brilliant editor, he is also a passionate cook; and during the time we spent together editing the film he often took over my kitchen and created some memorable meals for us. However, when I asked him for some of his recipes to include in this book, he argued that his recipes were traditional Italian ones that he couldn't take any credit for inventing, and so they had no place in a book of original recipes. I argued back that all good cooks have their own way of cooking traditional food that makes it uniquely their own. For example, if I were making this dish I would probably be inclined to add a half-inch piece of grated ginger root during the cooking.

Preparation time: 45 minutes

Serves 4

> 3 tablespoons olive oil
> 2 garlic cloves, peeled and chopped
> 2 dried red chili peppers
> 1 chicken (about 3 pounds), skinned and cut into serving pieces
> ½ cup wine vinegar
> About 1 tablespoon dried rosemary leaves
> Salt to taste
> Ground black pepper to taste

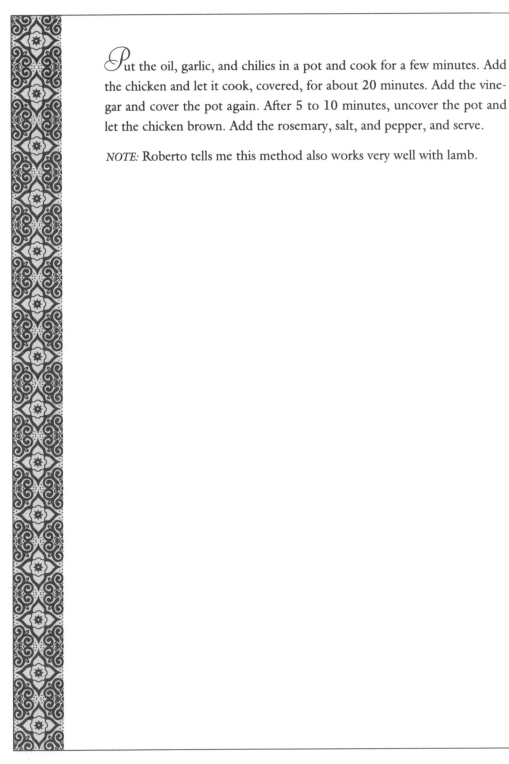

𝒫ut the oil, garlic, and chilies in a pot and cook for a few minutes. Add the chicken and let it cook, covered, for about 20 minutes. Add the vinegar and cover the pot again. After 5 to 10 minutes, uncover the pot and let the chicken brown. Add the rosemary, salt, and pepper, and serve.

NOTE: Roberto tells me this method also works very well with lamb.

Dahi-walli Mursh Kalejee
Chicken Livers Baked in Spicy Yogurt

Preparation time: 50 minutes

Serves 4

1 teaspoon ground black pepper
1 fresh hot green chili, seeded (optional) and chopped fine
4 garlic cloves, peeled and chopped
¼ teaspoon salt
2 tablespoons softened butter
1 cup plain yogurt
1 pound chicken livers

Combine the black pepper, chili, garlic, and salt with the butter in a small ovenproof dish. Stir in the yogurt and mix well.

Add the chicken livers and marinate for 15 minutes.

Meantime, heat the oven to 325°F. Place the dish in the oven and bake for 30 minutes, until the livers are cooked through, basting frequently with the yogurt sauce. Serve with Raw Spinach Salad (page 52) and Yellow Turmeric Rice (page 133).

Rai-walli Murgh Kalejee
Chicken Livers Baked in Spicy Mustard

◈

Preparation time: 50 minutes

Serves 3–4

 ½ cup plain or flavored Dijon mustard
 1 teaspoon ground black pepper
 4 garlic cloves, peeled and chopped
 2 tablespoons chopped parsley
 1 teaspoon cumin seeds
 2 tablespoons softened butter
 1 pound chicken livers

Combine the mustard, pepper, garlic, parsley, cumin, and butter in a small ovenproof dish. Add the chicken livers and let them marinate for 15 minutes.

Heat the oven to 325°F. Place the dish in the oven and bake for 30 minutes, until the livers are done, basting frequently with the mustard sauce. Serve with rice.

Bathak Mussallam
Roast Stuffed Duck

Preparation time: about 2½ hours

Serves 2–3

1 oven-ready duck, about 5 pounds, with giblets
Salt
Stuffing (see page 170)
2 garlic cloves, peeled and crushed
Ground black pepper

Heat the oven to 350°F. Wash the giblets and set them to simmer in water to cover for 20 or 30 minutes to make a stock.

Meanwhile, wash the duck thoroughly, then dry it. Remove any visible fat from the neck and body cavity.

Rub the cavity of the duck with salt, then fill with stuffing and truss the duck (see Note).

Rub the skin with the crushed garlic and sprinkle with 1 teaspoon or more of pepper. Prick the breast with a fork to release the fat during cooking.

Place the bird on a rack in a roasting pan and roast for 2 hours, until the juices run clear. Baste often with the drippings and some of the giblet stock.

Cut the duck into quarters and serve the stuffing and the rest of the warmed stock separately. Serve with Endive Walnut Salad (page 50).

NOTE: To truss the duck, pass a skewer through one wing of duck, then through the neck flap and the other wing. Tie the legs together.

Khas Bathak Masala

Ismail's Duck Stuffing

Preparation time: 5 minutes

Enough for a 5-pound duck

3 tablespoons mustard
2 tablespoons vinegar
1 cup dried bread crumbs
1 dried red chili, seeded (optional) and finely chopped
6 garlic cloves, peeled and chopped
1 apple, peeled, cored, and sliced
½ teaspoon salt

Combine the mustard and vinegar and stir in the bread crumbs. Add the chili, garlic, apple, and salt; toss together until well mixed.

Qaaz Mussallam
Roast Stuffed Goose

◈

One Christmas we had a big crowd, so I prepared two geese. They aren't as difficult to cook as one might think—and they are delicious. They may make turkey seem rather bland by comparison.

Prepare the goose for roasting as you would a turkey, except you really must place it on a rack or trivet as it produces lots of fat while cooking. Prick the skin to release the fat during roasting.

Preparation time: about 4½ hours

Serves 8–10

1 oven-ready goose, about 12 pounds
Salt
Spicy Fruit Stuffing (see page 172)
2 tablespoons ground black pepper (approximately)

Heat the oven to 325°F. Wash the goose thoroughly, dry it, and weigh it. Rub the cavity of the goose with salt and fill it with the stuffing. Place it on a rack or trivet in a large roasting pan.

Using a fork, prick the goose all over the breast and legs. Sprinkle with *lots* of black pepper.

Roast for 20 or 25 minutes a pound, checking from time to time to spoon off the excess melted fat. (Cool, then refrigerate this superbly flavored fat to use in cooking other dishes.)

Serve the goose and stuffing with roast potatoes and a dressed green salad.

Phal-walli Qaaj Mussallam
Spicy Fruit Stuffing for Goose

Preparation time: 10 minutes

Enough for a 12-pound goose

1 cup dried bread crumbs
6 small whole crabapples
3 pears, peeled, cored, and coarsely chopped
1 cup raisins
1 tablespoon chopped parsley
½ cup mustard
Salt to taste
1 tablespoon ground red pepper
½ pound potatoes, cooked and mashed
½ cup chicken or goose giblets, chopped (see Note)

Combine all the ingredients in a large bowl.

NOTE: Or use whatever leftover meat you find in the refrigerator. Chopped Meat with Peas Kashmiri-Style (page 209), for example, goes very well.

Feelmurgh Mussallam
Roast Stuffed Turkey

In the United States my friends invariably want turkey for Thanksgiving. It's always good, but turkey can sometimes be rather bland, so I make a spicy dressing to increase the pleasure of roast turkey.

Preparation time: 4¼–5¼ hours

Serves 12–16

> 1 oven-ready turkey, 12 to 15 pounds, with giblets
> Salt
> Spicy Turkey Stuffing (see page 174)
> At least 1 tablespoon freshly ground black pepper
> Vegetable oil (optional)

Wash the giblets and simmer them in enough water to cover 20 to 30 minutes to make a stock.

Heat the oven to 325°F. Wash the bird thoroughly, then dry and weigh it.

Rub the cavity with salt and fill with the stuffing. Some cooks insist on sewing up the opening, but I am always in such a rush I don't have time.

Sprinkle lots of black pepper all over the turkey. To prevent the turkey from drying, cover it with cheesecloth moistened in vegetable oil or the giblet stock to hold in the moisture.

Roast the turkey for 20 minutes a pound, basting frequently with vegetable oil or the giblet stock.

Tez Feelmurgh ka Masala
Spicy Turkey Stuffing

Preparation time: 10–15 minutes

Enough for a 12–15-pound turkey

Turkey giblets, cooked and chopped
2 fresh hot green chilies, seeded if desired and coarsely chopped
2 medium onions, peeled and coarsely chopped
¼ cup tarragon vinegar
¼ cup olive oil
6 garlic cloves, peeled
3 tablespoons chopped parsley
4 dried red chilies, seeded if desired
1½ cups dried bread crumbs
2 tablespoons chopped walnuts
2 tablespoons raisins

Combine giblets, green chilies, onions, tarragon vinegar, olive oil, garlic, parsley, and red chilies in a food processor. Coarsely chop the mixture.

Blend the bread crumbs thoroughly into the giblet mixture, then stir in the walnuts and raisins.

Meat—
a Whole New Gastronomic Chapter

Muslims are great meat eaters, and at home meat was part of our daily diet. Generally we had goat, which is the commonest meat in India, although we also ate lamb and beef. But it wasn't until I came to the West that I discovered the vast range of meat available, and the variety of cuts that each animal can provide. There must be at least ten varieties of beefsteak alone.

Not only did this open up a whole new gastronomic chapter for me but, when I began to cook, meat became—and continues to be—a source of great inspiration. Even after all this time, it wasn't until 1985, when we were shooting <u>A Room with a View</u> in Florence, that I tasted for the first time the famous Bistecca Fiorentina, huge chunks of steak cooked over wood, which gives it its distinctive flavor.

Veal was another great discovery for me. In India, the Hindus (the majority of the population) consider the cow to be a sacred animal and not for eating. Even for us, beef was a great treat, though in India it comes from water buffalo and bulls. So tasting veal for the first time was a wonderful experience. It's so tender and delicious, with a subtle flavor that lends itself to all kinds of adaptation.

I love going to really good butchershops in New York and London and Florence and, especially, Paris, where the meat is always so beautifully prepared. I rarely eat meat every day, but when I do choose to have meat I always buy the best and cook it carefully. Meat should always be tender and juicy—never overcooked or dried out.

Phasli ka Taj
Crown Roast of Lamb, Merchant-Style

❖

Preparation time: 45 minutes, plus roasting

Serves 10 (2 ribs per person)

3 racks of lamb, each with 6 to 8 ribs, making a total of 20 ribs

FOR THE STUFFING:

¾ pound chopped lamb, approximately
½ cup fresh white bread crumbs
Juice of 2 lemons
4 or 5 scallions, finely chopped
½ pound shelled fresh chestnuts, chopped (or canned unsweetened
    chestnuts, drained and chopped, or shelled walnuts)
Salt and freshly ground black pepper to taste

FOR THE RUB:

Juice of 1 lemon
1 tablespoon chopped parsley
1 teaspoon salt
1 teaspoon ground black pepper
1-inch piece of fresh ginger root, peeled and grated

Have the butcher trim away the skin from the racks, then cut the meat
from the tops of the bones and have this chopped to use for the stuffing.
Weigh the racks to calculate cooking time.

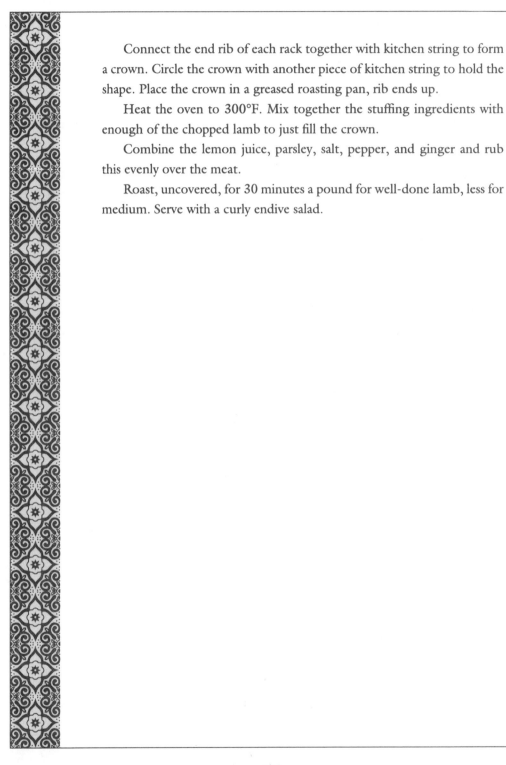

Connect the end rib of each rack together with kitchen string to form a crown. Circle the crown with another piece of kitchen string to hold the shape. Place the crown in a greased roasting pan, rib ends up.

Heat the oven to 300°F. Mix together the stuffing ingredients with enough of the chopped lamb to just fill the crown.

Combine the lemon juice, parsley, salt, pepper, and ginger and rub this evenly over the meat.

Roast, uncovered, for 30 minutes a pound for well-done lamb, less for medium. Serve with a curly endive salad.

Adrak aur Shazeera-walli Ran

Roast Lamb with Ginger and Caraway

❖

Raquel Welch enjoyed this particular dish, which I prepared for her just before we began shooting *The Wild Party*.

Preparation time: about 2 hours plus marinating

Serves 6–8

FOR THE MARINADE:

½ cup lemon juice
2 fresh hot green chilies, seeded (optional)
6 dried red chilies, seeded (optional) and chopped
2-inch piece of fresh ginger root, peeled and chopped
1 teaspoon chopped parsley
1 tablespoon caraway seeds
3 large garlic cloves, peeled

Salt
1 leg of lamb, about 7 pounds, trimmed
2 tablespoons chopped parsley

Purée the marinade ingredients in a food processor until smooth.
   Add salt to taste, then rub the marinade over the lamb on all sides. Let the meat stand at room temperature to season for 1 to 2 hours.
   Heat the oven to 450°F.
   Place the lamb and marinade in a greased baking pan, sprinkle with

the parsley, and sear the meat in the oven for 30 minutes.

Reduce the heat to 400°F and roast for 1 hour longer, for medium meat. Allow the meat to rest for 15 minutes, then slice and serve with warmed pita bread and Cucumber Raita (page 16).

Bhuna Gosht
Pan-Roasted Lamb

❖

Preparation time: 1½ hours, plus marinating

Serves 12

4½ pounds boneless lean leg of lamb (about 7 pounds before boning
   and trimming)
2 tablespoons finely chopped fresh ginger root
3 fresh hot green chilies, chopped with seeds
1 tablespoon finely chopped garlic
1½ tablespoons chopped coriander leaves
Juice of 1 lemon
Salt to taste
1 teaspoon ground black pepper
1 tablespoon vegetable oil

Cut the meat into 1½-inch cubes and place in a bowl. Combine the ginger, chilies, garlic, coriander, lemon juice, salt, pepper, and oil, and mix with the lamb. Set aside to marinate in the refrigerator at least 1 hours, or until you are ready to cook.

Heat the oven to 350°F.

Put the lamb and its marinade in a shallow roasting pan measuring about 9 × 13 inches. Bake, uncovered, for 1¼ hours without stirring. The lamb should be tender with plenty of pan juices.

Serve with Basmati Pilaf (page 132) and a curly endive salad.

Masala Gosht Seenghdar
Lamb Chops

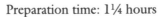

Preparation time: 1¼ hours

Serves 6

    2 pounds shoulder lamb chops

    1 large onion, peeled and sliced thin

    3 large garlic cloves, peeled and sliced thin

    1½-inch piece of fresh ginger root, peeled and grated

    1 fresh hot green chili, sliced in half lengthwise, seeded if
        desired

    2 teaspoons salt, or to taste

    3 (2-inch) pieces cinnamon sticks

    3 or 4 whole black cardamom pods, lightly crushed

    2 teaspoons garam masala

    6 or 7 whole cloves

    A pinch of turmeric

    4 medium tomatoes, or 6 ounces canned tomatoes,
        drained and chopped

    3 tablespoons plain yogurt

    ½ bunch chopped fresh coriander leaves

Arrange the chops, with the onion, in a large skillet over low heat. Add the garlic, ginger, chili, salt, cinnamon, cardamom pods, garam masala, cloves, and turmeric. Simmer (note: no oil) over medium heat, turning frequently, until the onions are soft and the juice is running from the chops.

After 15 or 20 minutes add the chopped tomatoes, yogurt, and coriander. Stir well, and simmer gently until tender (about 45 to 60 minutes). Add up to 1 cup of water if it becomes dry.

Serve the chops on heated plates topped with the sauce.

Rajasthani Gosht
Rajasthani Spicy Lamb Stew

❖

Preparation time: 1¾ hours

Serves 4

¼ cup vegetable oil
1 pound boneless lean lamb, cut into 2-inch cubes
2 medium onions, peeled and sliced
1-inch piece of fresh ginger root, peeled and chopped
8 garlic cloves, peeled and chopped
1 teaspoon ground coriander
½ teaspoon ground cumin
½ teaspoon turmeric
½ cup plain yogurt, stirred
2 teaspoons ground red pepper
Salt to taste

Heat half the oil in a heavy skillet over medium-high heat. When hot, add the cubed lamb and brown on all sides. Remove the meat with a slotted spoon and reserve.

Add the rest of the oil to the pan. When hot, add the onions and brown them, stirring frequently to prevent burning.

Meanwhile, mix the ginger, garlic, coriander, cumin, and turmeric into the yogurt. When the onions are browned, add the meat and yogurt mixture to the pan, stirring. Reduce the heat to medium-low and simmer for 10 minutes, adding a little water if necessary to prevent burning.

Stir in the red pepper, season with salt, and add 1¾ cups hot water. Cover, lower the heat, and simmer for 1¼ hours, until the meat is tender and the spicy gravy is thick. Serve with plain boiled rice.

Palak Gosht
Lamb with Spinach

Preparation time: 1½ hours

Serves 6–8

 4 tablespoons (½ stick) butter
 2 tablespoons vegetable oil
 2 medium onions, peeled and sliced thin
 4 garlic cloves, peeled and crushed
 4 teaspoons garam masala
 ½ teaspoon ground red pepper
 ½ teaspoon ground black pepper
 2-inch piece of fresh ginger root, peeled and grated
 2 pounds boneless lamb, cut into 1-inch cubes
 1 teaspoon salt, or to taste
 1½ pounds spinach, washed and chopped

Melt the butter with the oil in a heavy saucepan over medium heat. Add the onions and garlic and brown for about 1 minute. Add the garam masala, red and black pepper, and ginger, stir, and cook for 2 minutes. Add the meat and blend in well. Season with salt. Cook for 20 minutes, stirring frequently.

Add the spinach, stir well, cover the saucepan, and simmer 30 minutes longer, or until the lamb is tender and the spinach is well blended in.

Tamatar Gosht

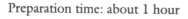
Lamb in Tomato Sauce

❖

Preparation time: about 1 hour

Serves 6–8

2 pounds boneless lamb, cut into 1-inch cubes

2 medium onions, peeled and sliced

1 tablespoon garam masala

¼ teaspoon turmeric

½ teaspoon ground red pepper

2-inch piece of fresh ginger root, peeled and grated

5 or 6 garlic cloves, peeled and crushed

2 teaspoons salt

1-inch piece of cinnamon stick

3 cardamom pods, lightly crushed

1 fresh hot green chili, seeded and chopped

1½ pounds tomatoes

Chopped fresh coriander leaves, for garnish

Place the meat in a saucepan over medium heat and add the onions, garam masala, turmeric, red pepper, ginger, garlic, salt, cinnamon stick, cardamom pods, and chili. Simmer gently for 15 to 20 minutes, until the onions have softened.

Chop the tomatoes roughly and purée them in a food processor. Add this to the simmering meat. Stir well, cover, and cook for 30 to 40 minutes, or until the lamb is very tender. You should have a rich tomato gravy. Serve garnished with coriander leaves.

Tamatar Gosht
Tomato Lamb Curry

❖

Preparation time: about 1½ hours

Serves 3–4

¼ cup vegetable oil
3 bay leaves, crumbled
1-inch piece of cinnamon stick
4 whole cloves
4 cardamom pods
4 peppercorns
1 pound boneless lean lamb, cut into large bite-size pieces
1 large onion, peeled and grated
½ teaspoon ground ginger
½ teaspoon finely chopped garlic
¼ teaspoon turmeric
½ teaspoon ground coriander
1 teaspoon ground red pepper
½ teaspoon salt
1 large tomato, chopped fine
1 tablespoon chopped fresh coriander leaves

Heat the oil in a heavy skillet over medium heat. When hot, add the bay leaves, cinnamon, cloves, cardamom pods, and peppercorns and cook until they begin to pop, 2 to 3 minutes.

Add the lamb and onion and cook, stirring, until the onion and the lamb are lightly browned.

Stir in the ginger, garlic, turmeric, ground coriander, red pepper, and salt. Turn the heat to medium-low and cook for 3 to 4 minutes.

Add the chopped tomato to the mixture, stirring well, and cook for 5 minutes, until the tomato becomes very soft.

Add 1¾ cups hot water to the pan, bring to a boil, cover, and simmer over low heat for 1 hour, or until the meat is tender. Stir in the chopped coriander leaves and serve with Basmati Pilaf (page 132).

Gosht Pillau
Lamb and Rice

❖

This recipe appears long and complicated, but it's really very easy to prepare.

Preparation time: 2 hours

Serves 12–14

FIRST STAGE:

   3 pounds boneless lamb, cut into 1-inch cubes
   1 medium onion, chopped
   6 or 7 garlic cloves, peeled and chopped
   2-inch piece of fresh ginger root, peeled and grated
   2 tablespoons garam masala
   2 teaspoons salt
   2 whole dried red chilies
   ½ teaspoon turmeric
   Juice of 1 lemon

Put the lamb in a large, heavy saucepan with the onion, garlic, ginger, garam masala, salt, chilies, turmeric, and lemon juice. Add 8 cups of water and bring to a boil. Cook over medium heat, covered, for about 1½ hours, until the meat is tender. Drain through a sieve and reserve the stock. Set aside the meat and discard the rest of the ingredients.

Second stage:

    3 tablespoons vegetable oil
    1 medium onion, peeled and chopped
    1 teaspoon cumin seeds
    2 tablespoons plain yogurt
    3 cups basmati rice, washed 3 or 4 times and soaked in cold water
      for half an hour
    2 teaspoons salt

In a large, heavy saucepan, heat the oil and cook the onion until golden brown. Add the cumin seeds and the reserved lamb and cook for 5 minutes. Add the yogurt and cook for a further 5 minutes. Add the rice, salt, and 5 cups of the reserved stock. (If there is not enough stock, supplement it with water.)

Cover the saucepan with a clean linen kitchen towel and then the lid. Bring the mixture to a boil and remove the lid and towel. Give it one good stir, and let it simmer over very low heat, covered, for approximately 20 minutes, until all the liquid is absorbed and the rice is cooked through.

Third stage:

    A few strands of saffron

Soak a few strands of saffron in 2 tablespoons of water, pour it over the top, and stir it gently into the rice.

Kaju Gosht
Lamb and Cashew Stew

Preparation time: 1½–2 hours

Serves 5–6

FOR THE LAMB STEW:

> ½ cup vegetable oil
>
> 2 pounds boneless lean lamb, cut into large bite-size pieces
>
> 8 medium onions, peeled and chopped fine
>
> ½ teaspoon salt
>
> 8 whole cloves
>
> 8 peppercorns
>
> 3 cinnamon sticks
>
> 1 tablespoon caraway seeds
>
> 1 tablespoon cumin seeds
>
> 4 or 5 bay leaves
>
> 1 cup plain yogurt
>
> 8 to 10 garlic cloves, peeled and crushed
>
> 3 tablespoons finely chopped fresh coriander leaves

FOR THE CHILI PASTE:

> 10 to 15 fresh hot green chilies, seeded
>
> ¼-inch piece of fresh ginger root, peeled
>
> 6 garlic cloves, peeled

FOR THE CASHEW PASTE:

4 ounces cashews
3 tablespoons sesame seeds
3 tablespoons poppy seeds

*P*repare the lamb stew: Heat one-third of the oil in a large heavy saucepan over high heat. When hot, add the lamb, in batches to avoid crowding, and cook, stirring frequently, until it is browned on all sides, about 5 minutes. As it browns, remove the lamb from the pan with a slotted spoon and reserve.

Turn the heat to medium, add half the remaining oil and the onions, and cook, stirring frequently, until the onions soften, 7 or 8 minutes.

Return the lamb to the pan with the salt, cloves, peppercorns, cinnamon sticks, caraway, cumin, and bay leaves. Add enough hot water to cover. Bring to a boil, then simmer for 25 minutes, until the meat is cooked through but not tender. Drain and reserve the broth and return the mixture to the pan.

Meanwhile, make the chili paste by processing the chilies, ginger root, and garlic to a paste in a food processor, or in batches in a blender, and reserve. For the cashew paste, purée the cashews and seeds similarly and reserve.

Add the chili paste to the lamb and gently simmer the mixture over low heat for 10 to 15 minutes, adding a few spoonfuls of the reserved broth as necessary to prevent burning.

Add the cashew paste and simmer for another 10 to 15 minutes, adding broth as necessary.

Add the yogurt and let it simmer for 5 minutes.

Add broth or water according to the thickness of sauce you desire. Simmer gently until the meat is tender, adding a little more liquid as necessary.

Heat the rest of the oil in a small saucepan over medium-low heat and add the garlic. When the garlic is golden, add it to the stew with the coriander, cover immediately, and cook gently for 5 more minutes. Uncover just before serving. Serve with Saffron Pilaf (page 131).

Ismail Merchant's Passionate Meals

Keema Matar
Minced Meat with Peas

❖

Preparation time: 25–30 minutes

Serves 6–8

3 tablespoons vegetable oil
1 large onion, quartered and sliced
4 garlic cloves, peeled and chopped fine
1 tablespoon fresh ginger, peeled and grated
2 teaspoons garam masala
1½ teaspoons salt
½ teaspoon ground red pepper
¼ teaspoon turmeric
1 cinnamon stick
2 black cardamom pods, slightly crushed
1½ pounds ground lamb or beef
2 tablespoons plain yogurt
3 medium tomatoes, finely chopped
1 cup green peas, fresh or frozen
Handful of fresh coriander leaves for garnish

Heat the oil in a saucepan and cook the onion until golden brown.
Add the garlic, ginger, garam masala, salt, red pepper, turmeric, cinnamon
stick, and cardamoms. Cook all the spices for about 5 minutes over a low
flame.

Add the meat, stirring occasionally until it starts to brown. Add the yogurt, cook for another 10 to 15 minutes, and then add the tomatoes and peas. Cover the saucepan and simmer for another 15 to 20 minutes. Serve garnished with fresh coriander.

Bhuna Phasli
Beef Rib Roast, Merchant-Style

◈

Preparation time: 2½ hours, plus marinating

Serves 4

    4 pounds beef rib roast
    Freshly ground black pepper

FOR THE MARINADE:

    2-inch piece of fresh ginger root, peeled and chopped
    ½ cup lemon juice
    2 fresh hot green chilies, seeded (optional) and chopped
    6 tablespoons chopped parsley
    ½ teaspoon coarsely ground black pepper

Place the beef on a plate or platter that will fit inside the refrigerator. Generously grind pepper over the meat.

Put the marinade ingredients in a food processor or blender and process them into a paste. Spread the paste over the meat, cover well with plastic wrap, refrigerate, and leave to season for 4 to 24 hours.

Heat the oven to 350°F. Transfer the beef to a greased roasting pan and roast for about 1½ hours for rare and 2 hours for medium. Serve with plain boiled rice and Cucumber Raita (page 16).

Gayki Boti
Braised Beef Cubes

❖

Preparation time: 1–1½ hours

Serves 4

    3 pounds stewing beef, cubed
    3 medium onions, peeled and chopped
    ½ cup vegetable oil
    4 garlic cloves, peeled and chopped
    ¼ cup lemon juice
    2 teaspoons Dijon mustard
    1 teaspoon salt

Heat the oven to 400°F.

Combine all the ingredients with ½ cup water in a heavy casserole or ovenproof dish, and bake covered for 50 to 60 minutes, or until the meat is tender.

Serve with Raw Spinach Salad (page 52) and warmed pita bread.

Shemali Gaye ke Tukre Baygan-walla

North Indian Beef and Eggplant Casserole

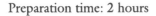

Preparation time: 2 hours

Serves 4–6

- 2 pounds lean ground beef
- 1½ cups plain yogurt
- ½ teaspoon salt
- ½ teaspoon ground black pepper
- 5 tablespoons olive oil
- 1 small eggplant, sliced
- 8 or 9 small whole scallions
- 1 green bell pepper, seeded and sliced
- 1 large tomato, sliced
- 4 or 5 dried red chilies, seeded if desired

Heat the oven to 375°F. Combine the beef, ¾ cup of the yogurt, half the salt, and half the pepper in a 1-quart soufflé dish or similar-sized ovenproof dish greased with 2 tablespoons of the olive oil.

Arrange the eggplant slices on top of the beef. For the next layer, cover with the scallions, using the bulbs plus 3 or 4 inches of the green stems.

For the next layers, spread the sliced green pepper, then the sliced tomato over the scallions.

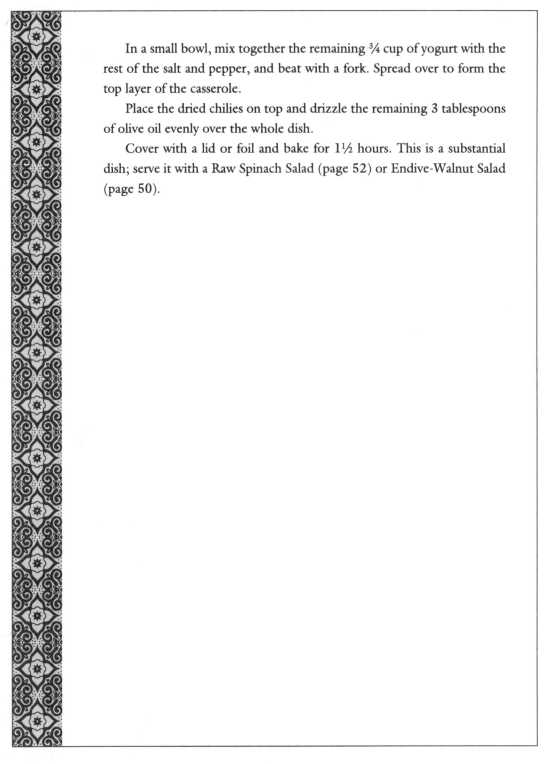

In a small bowl, mix together the remaining ¾ cup of yogurt with the rest of the salt and pepper, and beat with a fork. Spread over to form the top layer of the casserole.

Place the dried chilies on top and drizzle the remaining 3 tablespoons of olive oil evenly over the whole dish.

Cover with a lid or foil and bake for 1½ hours. This is a substantial dish; serve it with a Raw Spinach Salad (page 52) or Endive-Walnut Salad (page 50).

Kofta Curry
Curried Meatballs

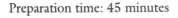

Preparation time: 45 minutes

Makes approximately 30

FOR THE MEATBALLS:

  1 pound ground lamb
  1 teaspoon garam masala
  ¼ teaspoon ground red pepper
  ½ fresh hot green chili, finely chopped
  Handful of fresh coriander leaves, chopped
  1 teaspoon salt
  1 teaspoon ground roasted chana dal (optional) (see Glossary)

FOR THE SAUCE:

  2 tablespoons vegetable oil
  1 medium onion
  3 garlic cloves, crushed or finely chopped
  4 medium tomatoes, finely chopped
  1½-inch piece of fresh ginger root, peeled and grated
  ½ teaspoon salt
  ½ fresh hot green chili, finely chopped
  ¼ teaspoon turmeric
  ¼ teaspoon ground red pepper
  ½ teaspoon garam masala
  Handful of fresh coriander leaves, for garnish

Kofta Curry (continued)

$\mathcal{M}$ix all the meatball ingredients together in a bowl until well blended. Set aside.

Begin making the sauce: Heat 2 tablespoons of oil in a large saucepan, add the onion and garlic, and cook gently over low heat until light brown. While the onions are browning, start making the meatballs. With wet hands, form the meat mixture into 1- to 1½-inch balls. This should make about 30 meatballs.

Add the tomatoes and ginger to the onions. Add the salt, chili, turmeric, red pepper, and garam masala and cook for 2 or 3 minutes, until thick. Add about ½ cup of water and turn down the heat. Add the meatballs, but do not stir. Cover the pan and simmer very gently for 10 or 15 minutes. You can shake the pan. When the meatballs are firm, stir gently and add about 2 cups of water. Simmer 15 or 20 minutes longer to thicken the sauce. Garnish with the coriander.

Shahi Kofta
Royal Kofta (Meatballs)

◆

Preparation time: 2½ hours

Serves 8

    2 pounds ground lean beef
    1¼ cups plain yogurt
    1½ teaspoons salt
    2 tablespoons finely chopped parsley
    1-inch piece of fresh ginger root, peeled and cut into small pieces
    5 fresh hot green chilies, seeded if desired
    6 garlic cloves, peeled
    ¼ cup lemon juice
    1½ teaspoons ground red pepper
    ¼ teaspoon turmeric
    ¼ teaspoon ground coriander
    ½ to 1 cup vegetable oil
    3 medium onions, peeled and chopped
    6 bay leaves, crumbled
    12 whole cloves
    A large pinch of saffron

Mix the beef with ¼ cup of the yogurt, 1 teaspoon of the salt, and the parsley. Set aside.

Combine the ginger, 3 of the chilies, the garlic cloves, and half the lemon juice in a food processor to make a paste. Transfer the paste to a bowl and add the red pepper, turmeric, and coriander.

Place the meat mixture in the food processor and add the remaining 2 tablespoons of lemon juice and 2 remaining chilies. Process until fairly fine.

With wet hands, form the mixture into 1½-inch balls.

Heat the oil in a large, thick-bottomed saucepan. Brown the onions over medium heat, stirring, then add the bay leaves and cloves.

Add the reserved paste to the hot browned onions, together with 1¼ cups hot water and the remaining ½ teaspoon of salt. Cook for 10 to 15 minutes over low heat. Add the remaining 1 cup of yogurt and cook for 5 more minutes.

Carefully add the meatballs to the sauce. They should be nearly submerged. Add the saffron.

Cover and cook slowly for 1½ hours. The meatballs should not break, but if some of them do, they will still taste fine. If you want to turn them, use a wooden spoon and do so gently.

Serve with Basmati Pilaf (page 132) and Lemon Lentils (page 102).

Chapli Kabab
Baked Spicy Beefburgers

❖

This is my version of the hamburger. It is baked, rather than fried or grilled, and it is a bit spicier than the usual burger.

Preparation time: 40 minutes

Serves 4–6

1½ pounds lean ground beef
¼ cup lemon juice
2 medium eggs
1 teaspoon ground red pepper
½ teaspoon salt
1 tablespoon finely chopped parsley

Heat the oven to 450°F. Mix all the ingredients together well and form the mixture into 4 to 6 patties.

Place them on a greased baking sheet and bake for 15 to 20 minutes. Serve with a good mustard and bread.

Adrak-walla Chapli Kabab
Gingerburgers

❖

Here's another version of my hamburger, with a surprise element of ginger.

Preparation time: 25 to 30 minutes

Serves 4–6

1½ pounds lean ground beef
2 medium eggs
¼ cup plain yogurt
1-inch piece of fresh ginger root, peeled and grated
1 fresh hot green chili, seeded (optional) and finely chopped
¼ teaspoon salt
1 or 2 garlic cloves, peeled and finely chopped

Heat the broiler. Combine all the ingredients thoroughly. Form the mixture into 4 to 6 patties and place them on the broiler pan.

Broil about 10 minutes, turning once, for rare meat, about 15 minutes for medium, and 18 to 20 minutes for well done. Serve with your favorite mustard and good bread.

Qeema Aloo Tikki
Spicy Beef Potato Cakes

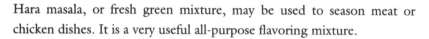

Hara masala, or fresh green mixture, may be used to season meat or chicken dishes. It is a very useful all-purpose flavoring mixture.

Preparation time: about 1 hour

Serves 4

FOR THE HARA MASALA (FRESH GREEN MIXTURE):

 1-inch piece of fresh ginger root, peeled and chopped
 4 garlic cloves, peeled and chopped
 2 fresh hot green chilies, seeded (optional) and chopped
 ¼ cup finely chopped parsley
 ¼ cup lemon juice
 ½ teaspoon ground black pepper

FOR THE BEEF MIXTURE:

 ¼ cup vegetable oil
 1 medium onion, peeled and chopped
 8 whole cloves
 1 pound lean ground beef

FOR THE POTATO PATTIES:

 4 large potatoes, freshly boiled
 1 tablespoon vegetable oil
 ¼ teaspoon salt
 1 teaspoon ground red pepper

2 tablespoons cream

3 large eggs

4 tablespoons butter

*F*irst, make the hara masala: Place the ginger, garlic, chilies, parsley, lemon juice, and black pepper in a food processor or blender to make a loose paste. Reserve the paste.

To make the beef mixture, heat the oil in a large skillet over medium-low heat. Add the onion and cloves and cook, stirring frequently, until onion is brown.

Add the meat to the pan, stirring, and cook until it starts to brown. After about 5 minutes, add the reserved masala paste. Cook over low heat for about 20 minutes, until the mixture is quite dry, stirring occasionally. Remove from the heat and reserve.

For the patties, peel the boiled potatoes and place them in a bowl. Mash them with a fork. (The potatoes have to be well mashed so they will make fairly thin patties. A blender may do the job well, but mashing by hand has worked well for centuries.) Mix in the oil, salt, red pepper, and cream. With your hands, make 8 round patties about 3 inches in diameter and ¼ inch thick or less.

Place a portion of the dry beef mixture on one patty, place another patty over it, and pinch the edges together gently to join them, making a sort of meat-filled potato dumpling.

Beat the eggs with a fork. Dip the patties into the beaten egg to coat them; this also helps hold them together.

Melt the butter in a skillet over low heat. Add the patties and fry them about 3 minutes on each side, turning once, until nicely browned. Serve with Tomato Mint Raita (page 20) and warmed pita bread.

Kashmiri Qeema Mattar
Chopped Meat with Peas Kashmiri-Style

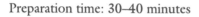

Preparation time: 30–40 minutes

Serves 2–3

> 1 pound lean ground beef or lamb
> Salt to taste
> ¼ teaspoon asafetida
> 1 cup plain yogurt, whisked
> 1½-inch piece of fresh ginger root, peeled and grated
> ½ cup vegetable oil
> 1 cup shelled green peas, defrosted if frozen
> 1½ teaspoons ground red pepper
> 1 teaspoon ground coriander
> ½ teaspoon ground allspice
> Handful of chopped fresh coriander leaves

Mix the ground beef or lamb, the salt, asafetida, yogurt, and ginger together in a bowl.

Heat the oil in a large skillet over medium-low heat. Add the meat mixture, stirring occasionally to break it up.

When the mixture begins to dry out, add the peas, red pepper, coriander, and allspice and cook until the meat is well browned, stirring continuously to prevent burning.

Add 1 cup of hot water, then gently simmer until the peas are cooked, about 10 minutes. (Shelled fresh peas will take 15 minutes or a little longer.)

Remove the mixture from the pan with a slotted spoon, transfer to a serving dish, and stir in the coriander leaves. Serve with Sherbanu's Rice (page 138) and Cucumber Raita (page 16).

Motlabai Sheekh Kabab
Spicy Chopped Beef Patties

Preparation time: 20–30 minutes

Serves 4

2 tablespoons butter
1 large onion, peeled and chopped
3 garlic cloves, peeled and chopped
1-inch piece of fresh ginger root, peeled and grated
1 teaspoon ground cumin
½ teaspoon ground cardamom
1 pound lean ground beef, lamb, or pork
3½ tablespoons dry bread crumbs
1 egg, beaten
3 tablespoons chopped fresh mint leaves
1 fresh hot green chili, seeded (optional) and chopped
¼ cup lemon juice
1 teaspoon salt
½ teaspoon ground red pepper
½ teaspoon ground black pepper
Vegetable oil for frying

Heat the butter in a frying pan over low heat. Add the onion and sauté for 3 minutes. Add the garlic, ginger, cumin, and cardamom; sauté the mixture, stirring occasionally, another 3 or 4 minutes and reserve.

Mix together the meat, bread crumbs, egg, mint, chili, lemon juice, salt, and red and black pepper. Add the onion mixture to the meat mixture and shape into patties about 2 inches in diameter.

Heat about ¾ inch of oil in a deep frying pan over medium heat. Add the patties two or three at a time, to give the oil time to reheat, and cook until the patties are well browned, turning them frequently. Remove patties with a slotted spoon and drain on paper towels. Serve with a mixed salad and warmed pita bread.

Ismail Merchant's Passionate Meals

Rai Adrak-walla Bachra
Roast Veal with Mustard and Ginger

❖

Preparation time: 3 hours 10 minutes, plus marinating

Serves 4–6

- 2 tablespoons vegetable oil
- 6 pounds loin of veal, boned and rolled
- 1 teaspoon ground red pepper
- 2 tablespoons Dijon mustard (preferably flavored with green pepper-corns)
- ½ cup lemon juice
- 1 teaspoon salt, plus extra for seasoning
- 3-inch piece of fresh ginger root, peeled and grated
- ¼ cup finely chopped parsley

Coat a roasting pan with the oil and place the veal in the pan.

Mix together the red pepper, mustard, lemon juice, and salt, and rub this over the veal.

Top the veal with the ginger, parsley, and a sprinkling of salt, and leave the meat to season in the refrigerator for 5 hours.

Heat the oven to 300°F. Bake the meat uncovered for 3 hours. Serve with rice.

Rai Gosht Masala
Veal with Mustard and Dill Sauce

❖

Preparation time: 1½ hours

Serves 4

1½ pounds boneless veal
½ cup plus 2 tablespoons olive oil
2 small onions, sliced
4 fresh bay leaves OR 2 dry bay leaves
1 large fresh hot green chili, chopped
2 garlic cloves, peeled and chopped
Juice of ½ lemon
1 tablespoon Dijon mustard
½ teaspoon salt
½ teaspoon ground red pepper
Handful of chopped fresh dill

Cut the meat into cubes. Heat ½ cup of the olive oil in a heavy saucepan. When hot add the onions and bay leaves. Cook for 1 or 2 minutes and then add the green chili and garlic. When the onions have browned, stir in the meat.

Mix together the lemon juice, the remaining 2 tablespoons of olive oil, and the mustard and make sure they are blended well. Sprinkle ½ teaspoon of salt over the meat, then add the mustard mixture and the red pepper. Let it cook, covered, over low heat for 1 to 1½ hours, or until the veal is tender. Transfer to a warmed serving dish and garnish with the chopped dill.

Joanna ka khas Gosht
Veal à la Joanna

This recipe was prepared in honor of my friend Joanna Rose.

Preparation time: about 1 hour

Serves 6 to 8

½ cup olive oil
2 onions, peeled and sliced
12 whole cloves
6 cardamom pods
2 pounds boneless veal, cubed
1-inch piece of fresh ginger root, peeled
2 dried red chilies
5 garlic cloves, peeled and chopped
Juice of 1 lemon
2 tablespoons plain yogurt
½ teaspoon salt, or to taste

Heat the oil in a large saucepan. Add the onions, cloves, and cardamoms. Cook for a few minutes until the onions start to soften. Add the veal to the pan. In a blender, make a paste of the ginger, red chilies, garlic, and lemon juice and add that to the veal. Add the yogurt, ½ cup of water, and ½ teaspoon of salt. Cover the pan and cook over medium heat for 30 to 45 minutes, or until the meat is tender.

FISH ON
THE TABLE

I love cooking with fish and eating fish. Without some kind of fish on the table I don't feel a meal is complete. I come from Bombay, on the Indian coast, which is a great fishing port, and so I grew up knowing about fish. My father would often take me with him to the fish stalls at Nul Bazaar, and he taught me how to recognize the freshness of fish: if a white substance forms at the gills, the fish is good, if red liquid forms, it isn't.

I grew up on exotic tropical fish—pomfret was a favorite—and never knew the cold-water varieties like salmon, haddock, halibut, and Boston scrod, or shellfish like langoustine and lobster, until I came to the West. As with meat, I am really excited by new discoveries. The first time I ate octopus was in Venice when we showed our film <u>Mr. and Mrs. Bridge</u> at the film festival there. I never thought I would be able to eat that strange-looking, rubbery thing, expecting it would be really disgusting, but when I tried it, I was amazed at how good it was.

Fish is quick and easy to cook, and very adaptable. You can have elaborate and adventurous sauces with it, but it's also excellent cooked very simply. Halibut, for example, cooked with capers, a little mustard sauce, and vinegar, takes only ten minutes and is a really fine dish. Thin slices of smoked salmon with a few capers, lemon juice, and crushed black peppercorns make the easiest and most terrific starter.

Machli Dam Masala
Cod in Tomato and Basil Sauce

❖

Preparation time: 40 minutes

Serves 12

3 pounds skinless, boneless cod fillets
3 tablespoons vegetable oil
1 large onion, grated
4 garlic cloves, peeled and crushed
1 teaspoon cumin seeds
½ teaspoon ajwain seeds
1 pound tomatoes, chopped fine
1-inch piece of fresh ginger root, peeled and grated
1 fresh hot green chili, chopped fine
1½ teaspoons salt
½ teaspoon ground red pepper
Pinch of turmeric
1 tablespoon garam masala
½ teaspoon ground black pepper
Handful of fresh basil leaves

Heat the oven to 350°F. Rinse the fish and divide it into 12 portions. Arrange in a large shallow, lightly oiled baking dish.

Heat the oil in a medium saucepan, put in the onion and garlic, and stir until brown. Add the cumin and ajwain and stir for a few moments. Add the tomatoes, ginger, chili, salt, red pepper, turmeric, garam masala, and black pepper. Cook gently for 5 minutes, until well blended.

Pour the sauce over the fish and bake, uncovered, for 20 to 30 minutes, or until cooked through. Roughly chop or tear the basil leaves and sprinkle over the fish just before serving.

Hara Masala Wali Machli
Codfish in Coriander Sauce

❖

Preparation time: 1½ hours

Serves 6

    3 medium tomatoes
    ¼ bunch fresh coriander, trimmed of roots
    1-inch piece of fresh ginger root, peeled
    ¼ teaspoon ground red pepper
    1 small fresh hot green chili (optional)
    Juice of 2 lemons
    1½ teaspoons salt, or to taste
    ½ teaspoon ground black pepper
    6 codfish steaks, each the size of an individual portion
    3 tablespoons vegetable oil

In a food processor blend the tomatoes, coriander, ginger root, red pepper, chili, lemon juice, salt, and black pepper. Marinate the fish steaks in this sauce in the refrigerator for approximately 1 hour. Heat the oil in a large skillet and add the fish with the marinade. Cover and cook for approximately 5 minutes. Turn the fish, cover, and cook for another 5 to 7 minutes until cooked through.

Machli ka Tikka
Grilled Halibut

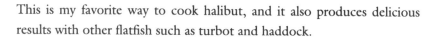

This is my favorite way to cook halibut, and it also produces delicious results with other flatfish such as turbot and haddock.

Preparation time: about 25 minutes

Serves 5–6

¼ cup lemon juice
3 pounds halibut steak, about 1½ inches thick, sliced into serving portions
3 tablespoons chopped parsley
½ teaspoon ground black pepper
Pinch of salt
3 garlic cloves, peeled and sliced thin
3 or 4 parsley sprigs, for garnish
3 or 4 lemon slices, for garnish

Heat the broiler. Position the rack so the fish will be about 7 inches away from the heat source. Rub the lemon juice into the fish. Coat both sides of the fish with chopped parsley, pepper, salt, and garlic. The garlic will adhere if sliced thin enough.

Place the fish in a foil-lined, then greased, baking pan. Broil for 8 minutes.

Turn the fish over and continue cooking for 8 minutes, or until the fish is done but not dry and overcooked.

Garnish with parsley sprigs and lemon slices. Serve with salad.

Naryal Machli ka Salan
Mackerel in Coconut Sauce

❖

Preparation time: 20 minutes

Serves 6

2 or 3 large whole mackerel or bluefish fillets (4 to 5 pounds in all), cleaned, discarding head and tail

1¾ cups Spicy Coconut Sauce (see opposite page)

Cut the fish into steaks of even thickness. Put the Spicy Coconut Sauce in a skillet and bring to the boil.

Add the fish steaks and simmer gently over lowered heat for 5 to 8 minutes, or until done. Serve with plain boiled rice.

Masaledar Naryal Salan
Spicy Coconut Sauce

Preparation time: about 50 minutes

Makes about 5 cups

1 coconut
1 medium dried red chili, seeded, cored, and chopped
6 garlic cloves, peeled and chopped
6 tablespoons chopped parsley
2 tablespoons ground black pepper
1 teaspoon salt

Heat the oven to 400°F. Pierce the coconut's eyes with a skewer and drain off the liquid. Place on an oven rack and bake for 15 minutes, or until the shell cracks. Place the hot coconut on concrete or another hard surface and smash it open with a hammer.

When the coconut pieces are cool enough to handle, peel away the brown papery skin from the white meat with a potato peeler. Chop any large pieces, if necessary, into smaller ones.

Put the coconut meat, the chili, garlic, parsley, pepper, and salt, along with ¾ cup of water, in a food processor or blender (in batches and with a little extra water if necessary) and process to liquefy the mixture.

Thin the coconut mixture with enough water to measure 5 cups of sauce.

Tamatar Walli Dum Machli
Baked Mackerel and Tomatoes

◆

Preparation time: 25 minutes

Serves 4–6

   2 or 3 mackerel (about 3¾ pounds), cleaned, discarding heads and
      tails
   ¼ cup vegetable oil
   1 tablespoon caraway seeds
   12 whole cherry tomatoes, OR 6 small tomatoes cut in half
   ¼ cup vinegar
   ¼ teaspoon salt
   1 teaspoon ground red pepper

Cut the fish crosswise into steaks, each about 1½ inches thick.

Heat half the oil in a large frying pan over low heat. Add the caraway seeds and cook for 3 to 4 minutes.

Add the mackerel steaks, then place the tomatoes on top of the fish.

Combine the vinegar, salt, the rest of the oil, and the red pepper and pour the mixture over the fish and tomatoes. Cover and cook over low heat for 15 minutes, or until the fish flakes easily when tested with a fork. Serve with Yellow Turmeric Rice (page 133).

Machli Lehsundar
Mackerel with Basil, Garlic, and Olive Oil

❖

Preparation time: 20 minutes

Serves 6

Juice of 1 lemon
1 cup olive oil
6 branches of fresh basil
8 or 10 garlic gloves, peeled (see Note)
1 teaspoon crushed black peppercorns
¼ teaspoon salt
6 small whole mackerel, cleaned (heads and tails attached)

Put the lemon juice, ¼ cup of olive oil, the basil leaves, garlic, pepper, and salt in a food processor and process to make a paste.

Cover the fish with the paste on both sides. Heat the remaining ¾ cup of oil in a frying pan and fry the mackerel for 5 minutes on each side. Cover the pan and continue cooking over low heat for a further 3 or 4 minutes, or until cooked through.

NOTE: The more garlic you offer your guests the better they will feel, because garlic is said to be very good for health.

Machli Muhammar
Grilled or Baked Red Mullet

❖

Preparation time: 15 minutes, plus marinating

Serves 8

8 small red mullet

FOR THE MARINADE:

Juice of 1½ lemons
½ teaspoon ground red pepper
1 teaspoon ajwain seeds OR oregano
2 teaspoons salt
½ teaspoon turmeric

FOR THE SAUCE:

3 tablespoons vegetable oil
5 garlic cloves, peeled and crushed
1 small can of tomato purée
7 small tomatoes, chopped
2½ teaspoons of fresh grated ginger root, peeled and grated
2 fresh hot green chilies
½ teaspoon ajwain seeds
¾ bunch fresh coriander leaves, washed
1½ teaspoons salt
Juice of 1 lemon
½ teaspoon ground black pepper

$\mathcal{C}$lean and wash the fish and scrape off all the scales. Mix all the marinade ingredients together and marinate the fish in the refrigerator for 1 hour.

Make the sauce: Heat the oil in a saucepan and add the garlic, stirring over medium-low heat until brown. Put the remaining sauce ingredients into a blender and blend until smooth. Pour into the oil and garlic and cook gently for 5 to 10 minutes.

EITHER: Grill or fry the fish and serve the sauce separately. This is good for a barbecue.

OR: Place the fish in a shallow baking dish and pour the sauce over the fish. Bake in a 350°F oven for 20 to 30 minutes, or until cooked through.

Teekhi Machli
Baked Porgies

❖

Preparation time: 35 minutes

Serves 4

- 4 porgies
- 6 plum tomatoes
- 2 large garlic cloves, peeled and chopped
- 1 tablespoon jalapeño mango mustard OR Dijon mustard
- 2 tablespoons olive oil
- 2 tablespoons vinegar
- Salt to taste
- A pinch of ground red pepper

Preheat the oven to 275°F. Rinse the fish and put them in a large baking dish. Cut the tomatoes in half and add them to the dish. Mix the garlic, mustard, olive oil, and vinegar, and pour over the fish on both sides. Sprinkle with salt and red pepper. Bake at 325° for about 25 minutes.

Rai Dar Machli
Mustard and Caper Salmon

◆

One evening, during the shooting of *Mr. and Mrs. Bridge* in Kansas City, Paul Newman telephoned and told me that a friend of his had brought him a huge fresh salmon from Alaska, and he invited me to go over to his house to cook it. I took Jim Ivory and Robert Sean Leonard, and we all went over to Paul and Joanna's house. Somehow, when I rang the doorbell I managed to set off all the alarms, and we couldn't turn them off. Paul and Joanna tore up and down the place trying to find whatever switch would disconnect the alarms, and we were all rushing around trying to help—except Jim, who is hopeless at mechanical things and just sat reading a magazine while all the chaos and noise was going on. Finally, Paul tore the wires out of the wall and killed the alarms.

Then we went into the kitchen, and there was this huge fish lying there. We decided that we should cut the fish in half—I would cook one half à la Merchant, and Paul, a famous cook, would cook his à la Newman. We both like very simple, quickly prepared food (in fact, Paul even suggested we should go into the restaurant business together). So he put his half of the fish on the barbecue with a little fresh lemon juice and ground black pepper. The recipe on the next page shows what I did with mine.

Mustard and Caper Salmon (continued)

Preparation time: 1 hour

Serves 8–10

   1 whole salmon (about 4 to 6 pounds), head and tail intact
   ¼ cup Dijon mustard, or garlic or tarragon, or other very good mustard
   ¼ cup good olive oil
   6 garlic cloves, peeled and chopped
   ¼ teaspoon ground red pepper
   Juice of 1 lemon
   1 teaspoon capers (preferably small)
   Salt to taste

Rinse the fish, pat it dry, then put in a baking pan that has been lined with foil and then greased. Mix together the mustard, olive oil, garlic, red pepper, lemon juice, capers, and a little salt. Coat the fish with this mixture on both sides and let it stand for 10 or 15 minutes, then bake uncovered at 375°F for 40 to 50 minutes, or until the flesh flakes easily at the touch of a fork.

Dum ki Lal Machli
Baked Red Snapper

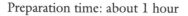

Preparation time: about 1 hour

Serves 3–4

> 2½ pounds red snapper, cleaned
> ¼ cup lemon juice
> 1 tablespoon caraway seeds
> 1 fresh hot green chili, seeded (optional) and sliced
> Salt and ground black pepper, to taste

Heat the oven to 350°F. Place the fish in a greased baking dish. Sprinkle 2 tablespoons of the lemon juice over the fish, then sprinkle with half the caraway seeds, half the sliced chili, and a pinch each of salt and pepper.

Turn the fish over and repeat with the remaining ingredients. Bake, uncovered, for 45 minutes.

NOTE: You can substitute smaller whole firm-fleshed fish such as mackerel in this recipe.

Kumbhi Dam ki Machli
Baked Trout in Mushroom Vinaigrette

◆

Preparation time: 35 minutes

Serves 3–4

    3 or 4 trout, each about ¾ pound, cleaned
    ¼ pound mushrooms, halved if very large
    1 tablespoon Dijon mustard
    2 tablespoons vinegar, lemon juice, or dry sherry
    1 tablespoon vegetable oil, plus extra for greasing and basting
    ½ teaspoon ground black pepper
    ¼ teaspoon salt

Heat the oven to 350°F. Arrange the fish and mushrooms in a greased baking pan. Whisk together the mustard, vinegar, and oil and pour the mixture over the trout and mushrooms.

Sprinkle the pepper and salt over the trout and bake for 20 minutes, basting with a little extra oil, until the fish is done. Serve with plain boiled rice.

Spaghetti aur Machli Roberto Silvi

Roberto Silvi's Spaghetti and Tuna

Preparation time: 45 minutes

Serves 4–6

    3 tablespoons olive oil
    1 whole head of garlic, the cloves separated, peeled, and chopped
    2 red bell peppers, seeded and chopped
    1 (12¼-ounce) can tuna in olive oil
    ⅓ tube anchovy paste
    ¾ large can tomatoes, chopped
    Large handful of chopped fresh parsley
    Salt to taste
    2 pounds of cooked spaghetti

Combine in a heavy saucepan the olive oil, garlic, bell peppers, tuna with its oil, anchovy paste, and tomatoes with their liquid. Cook over medium heat, stirring often so the tomatoes don't burn, for about 25 or 30 minutes. When the sauce is ready, add parsley and salt. Toss well into freshly cooked spaghetti.

This dish is traditionally eaten in Italy on Fridays, when Catholics used to be prohibited from eating meat. The prohibition has been lifted but the tradition lingers on.

Machli ka Salan
Spicy Fish Curry

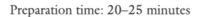

Preparation time: 20–25 minutes

Serves 4–6

1½ pounds cod or other whitefish steaks, skin removed
About 6 tablespoons vegetable oil
2 large onions, peeled, halved, and sliced thin
½ teaspoon ground coriander
¼ teaspoon turmeric
1 teaspoon ground red pepper
½ teaspoon ground ginger
6 garlic cloves, peeled and crushed or chopped very fine
1 large tomato, chopped
½ teaspoon salt
½ cup plain yogurt
1 teaspoon sugar

Cut the fish into large bite-size pieces. Heat 3 tablespoons of the oil in a skillet over medium heat. When hot, add the pieces of fish and lightly brown them on all sides, adding a little more oil if necessary. Remove the pan from the heat; remove the fish from the pan and reserve.

Heat 3 tablespoons of oil in the same pan over medium-low heat and when hot cook the onions until they are light brown, stirring occasionally.

Add the coriander, turmeric, red pepper, ginger, and garlic and cook for 2 to 3 minutes.

Add the tomato and salt and cook until the tomato is soft, adding water 1 tablespoon at a time if the spices stick. Stir in the yogurt and sugar and simmer gently for 5 minutes. Add the fish, stir well to heat through, and serve immediately with plain boiled rice.

NOTE: This curry is also good with mackerel, salmon, haddock, or mullet.

Dahi-walli Machli
Curried Fish in Yogurt

❖

Preparation time: 25 minutes

Serves 4–6

¾ cup vegetable oil

1½ pounds boned, skinned turbot, salmon, or other firm-fleshed fish
    cut into large bite-size pieces

2 large onions, peeled and grated

8 garlic cloves, crushed

1½-inch piece of fresh ginger root, peeled and grated

1 teaspoon cumin seeds

¼ teaspoon turmeric

1 teaspoon ground red pepper

1 cup plain yogurt

½ teaspoon salt

1 teaspoon sugar

⅛ teaspoon saffron powder

Heat ½ cup of the oil in a large skillet over medium heat. When hot, fry the pieces of fish in batches until they are lightly browned on all sides. Drain and reserve.

Add the remaining ¼ cup of oil to the pan and cook the onions over medium-low heat until they begin to turn golden. Add the garlic, ginger, cumin, turmeric, and red pepper and cook for 2 minutes.

Add the yogurt, salt, sugar, and saffron. Bring to a boil, lower the heat, and simmer gently for 10 minutes.

Add the reserved fish, cover, and cook for 2 or 3 minutes to heat it through. Serve immediately with Basmati Pilaf (page 132).

Masaledar Machli ke Unde
Ismail's Spicy Fish Roe

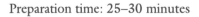

Preparation time: 25–30 minutes

Serves 6

2 pounds cod roe, in 1 piece
¼ teaspoon salt
¼ cup vegetable oil
1½ teaspoons ground black pepper
1 teaspoon cumin seeds
3 tablespoons Dijon mustard
½ cup lemon juice
2 teaspoons chopped fresh dill

Bring a large saucepan of water almost to a boil. Carefully add the roe with the salt, let the water return just to a boil, then lower the heat to a simmer.

When the roe begins to become firm (in 10 to 15 minutes), remove it from the water, draining in a colander. Place the drained roe in a bowl, mash it well, and reserve.

Heat the oil in a frying pan over medium-low heat. Add the black pepper and cumin seeds and cook for 30 seconds.

Stir in the mustard, then the mashed roe, lemon juice, and dill and cook for 5 to 10 minutes. Serve warm with a fresh salad.

Bare Jhingha aur Naryal Ka Salan

Coconut Lobster

You will remember this recipe for the rest of your life.

Preparation time: 30 minutes

Serves 4

2 live lobsters
The pulp from ½ coconut, peeled and cut into chunks
1 fresh hot green chili, seeded
3 garlic cloves, peeled
¼-inch piece fresh ginger root, peeled
6 stems fresh coriander, with leaves
2 tablespoons balsamic vinegar
¼ teaspoon salt
¼ cup olive oil
Chopped fresh coriander, for garnish

Boil the lobsters for 10 to 15 minutes in a large pot of salted water. When cool enough to handle, split them open and remove the tail and claw meat. Arrange on a serving plate.

To make the sauce, combine the coconut, chili, garlic, ginger root, coriander, vinegar, and salt in the container of a food processor and blend to a paste. Pour the paste evenly over the lobster and then drizzle the olive oil over the dish. Garnish with chopped fresh coriander.

Jhingha Nimbu
Jumbo Shrimp with Lemon and Ajwain

Preparation time: 20 minutes, plus marinating

Serves 4–6

    1 pound jumbo shrimp, cooked and shelled
    Juice of 1½ lemons
    ¾ teaspoon ajwain seeds
    1 teaspoon salt
    ¼ teaspoon ground red pepper
    ¼ teaspoon ground black pepper
    3 tablespoons vegetable oil

Marinate the shrimp in the lemon juice, ajwain seeds, salt, and red and black pepper for about 1 hour.

Heat the oil in a large skillet. Add the prawns with the marinade and cook over medium heat for about 5 minutes, or until heated through.

As a main course, serve these prawns with their sauce over rice. Drained, they are also good as a starter.

Tamatar Walla Jhingha
Jumbo Shrimp in Tomato Sauce

❖

Preparation time: 15 minutes, plus marinating

Serves 6–8

2 pounds jumbo shrimp, shelled (fresh or thawed frozen)
Juice of 1 lemon
½ teaspoon ajwain seeds
2 tablespoons vegetable oil
2 garlic cloves, peeled and crushed
3 small tomatoes, finely chopped
1-inch piece of fresh ginger root, peeled and grated
1 teaspoon salt, or to taste
Pinch of turmeric
¼ teaspoon ground red pepper
¼ teaspoon ground black pepper

Devein, and rinse the shrimp. Marinate in lemon juice and ajwain seeds for half an hour.

Heat the oil in a skillet, add the garlic, and cook for 2 minutes. Add the tomatoes, ginger, salt, turmeric, red and black pepper, and ½ cup water and simmer for 4 or 5 minutes. Add the prawns and their marinade and cook for 6 to 8 minutes or until just cooked through.

Sarson-walla Jhingha
Mustard Shrimp

◆

Preparation time: 15 minutes

Serves 4

¼ cup vegetable oil
½ teaspoon caraway seeds
½ teaspoon ground red pepper
1 pound raw shrimp, shelled, deveined, rinsed, and dried
1½ tablespoons Dijon mustard
¼ cup lemon juice
Salt to taste

Heat the oil in a small skillet over low heat. When hot, add the caraway seeds and red pepper and cook for 3 or 4 minutes.

Add the shrimp, mustard, lemon juice, and salt and stir well. Cover the pan and cook for 5 to 6 minutes.

Stir the mixture well and serve with Saffron Pilaf (page 131) and a green salad.

Jhingha Pullau
Shrimp Pilaf

❖

Preparation time: 50–60 minutes

Serves 6

1¾ cups basmati rice
1-inch piece of fresh gingerroot, peeled and grated
4 fresh hot green chilies, seeded (optional) and finely chopped
1 teaspoon ground red pepper
¼ teaspoon turmeric
¼ teaspoon ground coriander
8 garlic cloves, peeled and chopped fine
¼ cup lemon juice
¼ cup vegetable oil
2 medium onions, peeled and chopped
2 cinnamon sticks, broken into pieces
12 whole cloves
24 large shrimp, shelled, deveined, rinsed, and dried
¼ cup chopped parsley, to garnish

*P*ut the rice in a bowl and wash it in several changes of cold water. Cover it with plenty of fresh water and let it soak for 30 minutes.

Meanwhile, combine the ginger, chilies, red pepper, turmeric, coriander, garlic, and lemon juice to make a paste; reserve.

Heat the oil in a large, heavy-based saucepan over medium-low heat. When hot, add the onions, cinnamon, and cloves and sauté until the onions are beginning to brown, stirring occasionally.

Add the reserved paste to the sautéed onion mixture with ¾ cup of water and simmer for 8 to 10 minutes.

Add the shrimp and continue cooking over low heat for 2 minutes. Remove the shrimp from the pan with a slotted spoon and set them aside. Add 2½ cups of hot water to the spice mixture in the pan and bring to the boil.

Drain the rice well, then add it to the pan, stirring well. Cover the pan very tightly and cook over low heat for 15 minutes or until the water is absorbed.

Remove the pan from the heat, stir the reserved shrimp into the rice, cover, and let the shrimp finish cooking in the heat of the rice for 5 to 10 minutes.

Sprinkle with parsley and serve.

Dahi-walla Jhingha
Yogurt Shrimp

❖

Preparation time: 15 minutes

Serves 6

 ¼ cup vegetable oil
 4 garlic cloves, peeled and chopped
 1 tablespoon ground cumin
 ½ to 1 tablespoon ground red pepper
 ¼ teaspoon salt
 24 raw jumbo shrimp, shelled, deveined, rinsed, and dried
 1 cup plain yogurt

Heat the oil in a large skillet over medium-low heat. When hot, add the garlic, cumin, red pepper, and salt and cook for 5 minutes, or until the garlic begins to brown.

Add the shrimp and cook for 2 or 3 minutes, stirring.

Add the yogurt, stir, and continue cooking for 5 minutes. Serve with salad and boiled rice.

PICKLES AND CHUTNEYS—
Something of a Social Occasion

Pickles and chutneys are an essential accompaniment to every Indian meal, and in India are always homemade. Pickle making is something of a social occasion, and each family has its own recipes that have been handed down through the generations. In this chapter I have included some of my family's recipes. You will also find Hamida Begum's lime pickle recipe, which features so importantly in my film The Courtesans of Bombay. It is a very old recipe, originally for making in huge quantities, and is well worth the effort involved.

For me, pickles and chutneys serve an additional purpose: if I am alone and too tired or in too much of a hurry to cook, then a pickle sandwich with a bowl of good salad makes an ideal meal. I just heat up some French bread,

Ismail Merchant's Passionate Meals

slice it lengthways, rub it with garlic, then pile it with some tangy spicy pickle.

Use either glass or ceramic containers for pickles and chutneys. Choose fairly small jars if possible, that way the pickle is used up more quickly once opened. The jars must be thoroughly washed and sterilized with boiling water, and then dried off completely—putting them in a low oven (275°F) for 20 minutes or so is a good way of drying them.

It's best to put the pickle or chutney in the jar while it is still warm. Cover immediately with an airtight lid. Don't use metal lids for preserves containing vinegar.

When the preserve is cool, store in a cool dark place. Most will keep for six months unopened. Once opened, store the jar in the fridge and use up as soon as you can (within six weeks is best).

Pickles are hot and spicy, and chutneys are milder and sweeter. There is no hard and fast rule about which pickles or chutneys to serve with specific dishes—they're very adaptable. In most Indian households there are usually about ten jars of various pickles and ten jars of various chutneys, and you just pick whichever you want.

Sabji ka Aachar
Mixed Vegetable Pickle

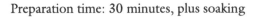

Preparation time: 30 minutes, plus soaking

Makes about 1½ pints

FOR THE VEGETABLES:

    1 medium cauliflower, cut into florets

    4 ounces green beans, topped and tailed

    1 medium carrot, cut into ¼-inch-thick slices

FOR THE MASALA PASTE:

    9 dried red chilies, seeded (optional) and chopped

    3 fresh hot green chilies, seeded if desired

    2-inch piece of fresh ginger root, peeled and grated

    2 teaspoons cumin seeds

    ½ teaspoon yellow mustard seeds

    ½ teaspoon ground fenugreek leaves

FOR THE PICKLING MIXTURE:

    1¼ cups distilled or white wine vinegar

    ¾ cup vegetable oil

    8 bay leaves, crumbled

    12 garlic cloves, peeled and coarsely chopped

    2 tablespoons sugar

    6 black peppercorns

    Coarse salt to taste

$\mathcal{M}$ix and wash the vegetables, then cover them with fresh cold water for 1 hour. Drain the vegetables well and leave them in a colander.

Grind the masala spices together with a mortar and pestle, adding a little vinegar (from the amount for the pickling mixture) to make a paste.

Make the pickling mixture: Heat the oil in a large nonreactive skillet over medium heat. When hot, add the bay leaves and garlic and cook, stirring frequently, for 2 or 3 minutes. Add the masala paste to the pan and fry for a further 5 minutes. Add the vegetables, sugar, peppercorns, salt, and the remaining vinegar. Cook over low heat until the vegetables soften.

Remove the mixture from the heat and let it cool. Transfer to clean glass or ceramic jars and cover with nonmetallic airtight lids. Store in the refrigerator.

Hara Dhania aur Podine ki Chutney
Mint and Coriander Chutney

Preparation time: 15 minutes

8 sprigs of fresh coriander, washed, coarsely chopped, and the root
    ends trimmed
Fresh mint leaves—4 times as much as the coriander
1 small onion, sliced
Juice of 1 lemon
1 fresh hot green chili, cored and coarsely chopped
1 teaspoon salt, or to taste
¼ teaspoon ground red pepper

Measure the coriander stems and leaves, loosely packed, in a large
measuring cup. Measure the mint leaves; rinse and dry them.

In the bowl of a blender or food processor, combine the coriander
and mint with the onion, lemon juice, green chili, salt, red pepper, and 2
tablespoons of water. Blend until the mixture is the consistency of tomato
ketchup. Serve immediately, or store in a jar in the refrigerator. This chutney goes well with pakoras.

Parveen ki Tamatar Chutni
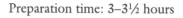
Parveen's Tomato Chutney

Preparation time: 3–3½ hours

Makes about 1¾ cups

   3½ pounds medium tomatoes, halved
   1¾ cups white wine vinegar
   ½ teaspoon coarse salt, plus additional as needed
   2 tablespoons raisins
   2-inch piece of fresh ginger root, peeled and finely grated
   1 garlic clove, peeled and crushed
   1½ teaspoons ground cumin
   ½ teaspoon cumin seeds
   8 whole cloves
   6 to 8 black peppercorns
   1 cinnamon stick, broken into pieces
   ½ cup sugar
   2 teaspoons ground red pepper

Wash the tomatoes, shake them dry, and put them in a large nonreactive saucepan with 1½ cups of vinegar and ½ teaspoon of salt. Cover and heat them until the vinegar boils, then reduce the heat and simmer uncovered until the tomatoes are barely tender, about 8 or 10 minutes. Remove them from the pan with a slotted spoon and set them aside to drain in a colander.

Meanwhile, soak the raisins in the remaining ¼ cup vinegar for at least 30 minutes.

Mix the ginger, garlic, and ground cumin to a fine paste. Mix in the cumin seeds and reserve.

Pound the cloves, peppercorns, and cinnamon stick together with a mortar and pestle.

Put the tomatoes in a dry nonreactive saucepan, add the sugar, and place over medium-low heat. Cook until the sugar melts, stirring occasionally. Add the garlic paste and the clove mixture to the pan. Stir in the raisins and their soaking liquid, and the red pepper. Cover and cook for 2 hours, or until the mixture is thick, stirring occasionally.

Remove the pan from the heat, add salt if desired, and allow the chutney to cool completely. Transfer to a clean glass or ceramic jar or jars, and cover with nonmetallic airtight lids. Store in the refrigerator.

Tamatar Chutni
Tomato Chutney

❖

Preparation time: 2¼ hours

Makes about 1½ pints

2 lemons
5 pounds tomatoes, quartered
1¼ cups white wine vinegar
1½ cups sugar
2 teaspoons ground red pepper
1 cup raisins
1 cinnamon stick, broken into small pieces
1⅓ cups slivered almonds

Seed and chop the lemons with their rinds, reserving the juice. Transfer the lemons and juice to a food processor, or in batches to a blender, and process them to shreds.

Combine the tomatoes, vinegar, sugar, red pepper, raisins, cinnamon, almonds, shredded lemons, and 2 cups of water in a deep nonreactive saucepan. Bring the mixture to a boil.

Reduce the heat and simmer, stirring occasionally, until almost all of the liquid has boiled away, about 2 to 2½ hours. (Watch carefully so the tomatoes do not burn. Use a flame tamer, or simmer over the lowest possible heat.)

Remove the chutney from the heat and let it cool. Transfer to clean glass or ceramic jars, and cover with nonmetallic airtight lids. Store in the refrigerator.

Ambia ki Chutni
Mango Chutney

❖

Preparation time: about 40 minutes, plus overnight maceration

Makes about 2 cups

2¼ pounds ripe mangoes
1¾ cups cider vinegar
3¼ cups dark brown sugar, firmly packed
Salt to taste
1½ teaspoons ground red pepper
1-inch piece of fresh ginger root, peeled and chopped fine
½ cup assorted dried fruit and nuts, such as golden raisins, currants, walnuts, dates, and cashews

Peel the mangoes and remove the seeds. Cut the flesh into slices. Place the slices in a glass jar or ceramic bowl and add the vinegar, brown sugar, salt, red pepper, and ginger. Stir well, cover, and let stand overnight.

The next day, transfer the mixture to a nonreactive saucepan and cook over low heat, stirring frequently, until the mixture begins to thicken.

Add the chopped fruit and nuts and continue cooking, stirring frequently to prevent burning, until the mixture is thick.

Remove the pan from the heat. When the chutney is cool enough, correct the seasoning with additional salt, red pepper, and vinegar.

Transfer the chutney to clean dry glass or ceramic jars and seal with nonmetallic airtight lids. Store in the refrigerator.

Bhare Nimboo ka Aachar
Hamida Begum's Stuffed Lime Pickle

◆

This recipe, which figures prominently in *The Courtesans of Bombay,* will produce enough pickle to last an entire family for quite a long time, as one can imagine. It is so good that there is always great demand for it from friends and family. You can, of course, reduce the quantities proportionately.

Preparation time: 2½ hours, plus cooling and bottling

Makes about 9¾ pints

  200 limes
  1¼ pounds dried red chilies
  1 cup mustard seeds
  ½ cup cumin seeds
  ½ cup onion seeds
  1 pound garlic, peeled
  1 pound coarse salt
  3¾ cups mustard oil
  12 fresh hot green chilies

Squeeze the juice from 100 of the limes into a large bowl; cover and reserve.

  Put the rest of the limes in a large nonreactive saucepot or preserving kettle, cover with plenty of cold water, bring to a boil, and simmer until they are tender. Drain the limes, dry them with a kitchen towel, and put them aside.

Take the red chilies and pound them fine with a mortar and pestle, or grind them in a food processor, or in batches in a blender.

Put the mustard, cumin, and onion seeds in a large skillet over low heat and dry-roast them for 2 or 3 minutes, shaking the pan occasionally. The seeds should begin to release their aroma.

Take two-thirds of the seed mixture and pound it fine with a mortar and pestle, or grind it in a food processor or in batches in a blender.

Combine the ground red chilies and the pounded or ground seed mixture with the remaining seed mixture.

Pound the garlic cloves into a paste with a little water, then drain off the water. Mix the garlic with the chili and seed mixture, adding the salt and a little of the lime juice to make a paste.

Cut each boiled lime halfway down into four sections. Spread the spice paste well into the limes, put them in a large container, and add the rest of the lime juice.

Warm the oil until it begins to sputter, then pour it over the stuffed limes and whole green chilies.

When the mixture is cool enough, transfer it to glass or ceramic jars and cover with nonreactive airtight lids. Store in the refrigerator.

Meethe Shaftaloo ki Chutni
Sweet Peach Chutney

Preparation time: about 3 hours

Makes about five 1¼-pint jars

    10 pounds firm ripe peaches
    2 cinnamon sticks
    1 cup medium-dry sherry
    6 cardamom pods
    1 pound sugar
    ¾ cup raisins
    ½ cup lemon juice
    1 teaspoon almond extract

Bring a large saucepan of water to a boil and remove it from the heat. Drop in 8 to 12 peaches and leave for 1 minute. Remove one peach at a time, peel off the skin, and set aside. Then halve and pit each peach and chop the flesh. Repeat with the remaining peaches.

Combine the peaches, cinnamon, sherry, cardamom pods, sugar, raisins, lemon juice, and almond extract in a large nonreactive saucepan. Bring the mixture to a boil, stirring frequently.

Reduce the heat and simmer uncovered over medium-low heat for 2 hours, or until the mixture becomes very thick, stirring frequently. Keep the heat as low as possible to prevent burning.

When the chutney is cool enough, transfer it to clean, dry glass or ceramic jars and cover with nonreactive airtight lids. Store in the refrigerator.

Phool Gobi ka Aachar
Cauliflower Pickle

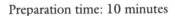

Preparation time: 10 minutes

Makes about 1¾ cups

  1 medium cauliflower, cut into florets
  1 fresh hot green chili, seeded (optional) and chopped
  5 to 10 garlic cloves, peeled and coarsely chopped
  1¼ cups white wine vinegar
  2 teaspoons coarse salt
  1 teaspoon turmeric
  1 teaspoon caraway seeds
  2-inch piece of fresh ginger root, peeled and coarsely grated
  1 tablespoon vegetable oil

Put all the ingredients and 1¼ cups of water into a large glass jar, and top with a nonmetallic airtight lid. Shake to mix well.

Allow the pickle to mature for 1 week in the refrigerator, shaking occasionally.

Aam Chhunda
Mango Relish

◈

Preparation time: about 1 hour

Makes about 1 pint

2¼ pounds hard green mangoes
2¼ pounds sugar
¼ cup coarse salt
5 or 6 black peppercorns
1½ teaspoons ground red pepper
2 or 3 black cardamom pods, coarsely pounded

Wash, dry, peel, and grate the mangoes into a large nonreactive saucepan.

Stir in the sugar and place the pan over low heat, stirring continually with a wooden spoon for about 30 minutes.

When the mixture changes color and falls into a thread when lifted with a spoon, remove the pan from the heat.

Stir in the salt, peppercorns, red pepper, and cardamom pods. Let the mixture cool.

Transfer the mixture to clean, dry glass jars and cover with nonreactive airtight lids. Store in the refrigerator.

Gobi aur Gazar ka Achar
Sherbanu's Carrot and Cauliflower Achar

This accompaniment should be freshly made; it does not keep for any length of time.

Preparation time: 15 minutes

Serves 4–6

3 cups sliced carrots and sliced cauliflower florets
½ teaspoon vegetable oil
¼ teaspoon turmeric
½ teaspoon ground red pepper
½ teaspoon sugar
2 tablespoons tarragon vinegar
½ teaspoon mustard seeds

Combine all of the ingredients and let the mixture sit for an hour or so, allowing the carrots and cauliflower to absorb the various flavors.

This can be served slightly cooled but not absolutely cold, as this would kill the flavor. Serve as a pickle or garnish.

Nimbu ka Achar
Sour Lemon Pickle

❖

Preparation time: ½ hour, plus 45 days to pickle

Makes 2 large jars

    4½ pounds large fresh lemons
    1 cup coarse salt
    1 tablespoon turmeric

Wash the lemons, wipe, and cut each into 8 wedges. Add the salt and turmeric. Mix and store in a clean glass jar. Stir every day.

In about 45 days the lemons will become soft and the pickle will be ready to eat.

BREAD—
a Part of One's Life

Bread is common all over India, and wherever food is prepared, whether at home or a roadside restaurant, there will be bread in one form or another. In northern India, bread and dal is the staple diet.

In the West, bread is made in bakeries, but in India the breads are made by the cooks at home or in restaurants at every meal as they are required, so bread is very much a part of one's life. There is a great variety of Indian bread, and the more economically sound you are the more sophisticated the bread you eat. The commonest bread is the chapati, a flat bread cooked on a skillet, which you find all over India. Then there are rotis, naans, parathas, and lachhe dar paratha, each with a vast number of variations.

You can create Indian bread in the kitchen with the greatest of ease, because it is not a complicated process or one that demands a lot of equipment. Breads like chapatis are cooked on a tava, a concave cast iron plate, but a skillet will do. Deep-fried breads like puris are cooked in a karhai, which is very like a wok. Indian breads have to be cooked very rapidly, like pancakes.

In India, breads are freshly prepared with each meal, the women love to serve warm breads to their husbands and sons, and the fresher the bread the better it is. I can easily eat two or three dozen puris or rotis at one time if they're freshly made. Of course, you can make as many rotis as you want and keep them fresh and moist by wrapping them in a napkin, consuming them as, and when, the meal is served.

In northern India, a typical breakfast is tea, a glass of yogurt drink, i.e., lassi, and paratha, a layered bread made with lots of butter or ghee so that it is very rich. In fact, the best parathas are often found in roadside stalls called dhaba, and these places are usually favored by lorry drivers because they know they can get good lassi and good parathas without fail.

Bhaturas
Fried Wheat Bread

❖

Preparation time: 40 minutes, plus 6–8 hours resting

Makes 10

1¾ cups all-purpose flour, plus extra for rolling
1¾ cups whole wheat flour
A pinch of salt
2 cups plain yogurt
1½ tablespoons baking soda
1 teaspoon sugar
Clarified butter or ghee (see page 299) for frying

Put the flours and salt in a bowl. Stir together the yogurt, baking soda, and sugar. Mix the yogurt into the flour to make a firm dough. Cover with a damp cloth and leave in a warm place for 6 to 8 hours.

Turn the dough out onto a lightly floured surface and knead briefly. Divide into 10 portions and roll each one into a 4-inch round. Melt some clarified butter or ghee in a heavy shallow frying pan and fry the dough rounds for 1 or 2 minutes on each side, until lightly browned. Drain on paper towels before serving.

Chapati
Flat Bread

Preparation time: 40 minutes, plus 30 minutes resting

Makes 15

1¾ cups whole wheat flour, plus extra for rolling

Put the flour in a bowl. Gradually add about ¾ cup of water, gathering the flour together with your fingertips to form a soft dough. Knead the dough for 6 to 8 minutes, until it is smooth. Put the dough in a bowl, cover with a damp cloth, and let it rest for 30 minutes.

Heat a griddle or heavy frying pan over medium-low heat for 10 minutes. When it is very hot, reduce the heat to low.

Knead the dough again briefly and divide it into 15 portions. It will be fairly sticky, so rub your hands with a little flour before handling it. Take one portion of the dough and form it into a ball. Flour the work surface generously, roll the ball in the flour, then flatten the ball slightly to make a patty. With a rolling pin, roll the patty out, dusting very frequently with flour, until it is about 5½ inches in diameter. Pick up the chapati, pat it between your hands to shake off extra flour, then slap it onto the hot griddle. Cook over a low heat for about 1 minute, until the underside develops brown spots. Turn the chapati over and cook for about 30 seconds on the second side.

Put in a warmed deep serving plate lined with a large napkin. Fold the napkin over the chapati and keep warm while making the rest.

Ideally, chapatis should be eaten immediately, but you can wrap the whole stack in foil and either refrigerate for a day or freeze. The chapatis may be reheated, still wrapped in foil, in the oven at 300°F.

Aloo Kulcha
Potato Bread

Preparation time: 60 minutes

Makes 15

> ½ pound (2 medium) potatoes, scrubbed
> 1½ cups all-purpose flour, plus extra for dusting the bread
> A pinch of salt
> Clarified butter, ghee, or vegetable oil for frying

Parboil the unpeeled potatoes in boiling water for about 15 to 20 minutes, until barely tender. Drain, cool slightly, then peel and grate into a bowl.

Add the flour to the potato with the salt and mix to form a soft dough, adding a little water if necessary. Divide the dough into 15 small pieces and dust with flour. Roll out each piece on a lightly floured surface into a 6-inch round.

Heat 2 or 3 tablespoons of clarified butter, ghee, or oil in a large shallow frying pan and fry the kulcha in batches, for 1 to 2 minutes, until tinged with brown, turning once. Drain on paper towels before serving.

Parathas

◆

Preparation time: 30 minutes

Makes about 16

3½ cups chapati flour (or whole wheat flour)
Soft butter, margarine, or vegetable oil for spreading
Vegetable oil for frying

*P*ut the flour in a bowl and gradually add 1 cup of cold water. Mix well with your hands until you have a stiff dough. Knead for 6 to 8 minutes, then let the dough rest for 10 or 15 minutes.

Divide the dough into 16 pieces and roll into balls about 2 inches across. Roll a ball into a 6-inch circle on a lightly floured work surface. Brush with a little soft butter. Dust with flour and shape into a 6-inch square. Fold the corners of the square into the center. Dust with flour and roll again into a round patty. Brush with butter, shape into a square, fold in the corners, and roll again. Roll all the balls this way.

Heat a tava, or heavy pan, for a minute or so. Lightly oil the pan and slap on a paratha. Cook for ½ to 1 minute. Turn and cook for 1 minute. Glaze with 1 teaspoon of oil. Turn again and spread another teaspoon of oil over the paratha. Push it around until the edges are cooked. Turn it again until it is lightly browned all over on both sides. When cooked, place on a plate and cover with foil to keep warm until you have cooked all the parathas this way.

Angreji Paratha
English Paratha

◆

During the time of the British Raj in India all the memsahibs (English ladies) had their khansama (cooks), whom they would instruct to prepare the native food in a certain way. In order to distinguish between the Indian and British way of preparing the food, the cooks referred to the Anglicized improvisations as "Angreji"—English.

Preparation time: 40 minutes, plus 30 minutes resting

Serves 8

> 2½ cups all-purpose flour
> 1 tablespoon salt
> Ghee (see page 299) or clarified butter
> 1 tablespoon butter

Sift the flour, and keep a small amount aside. Add the salt and 1 tablespoon of ghee to the flour with a little water to make a soft dough. Keep covered with a damp cloth for 30 minutes. Divide into 8 balls.

Roll out each ball thickly on a little flour. Spread some of the butter over it, and fold. Roll this out into an 8-inch circle, pressing lightly. Half fill the frying pan with ghee and fry the parathas on both sides until brown and crusty in hot ghee over medium heat, pressing them down into the ghee.

Puris

Preparation time: 15–20 minutes

Makes about 25

3½ cups whole wheat flour
½ teaspoon salt
1 tablespoon vegetable oil, plus additional for deep frying

Put the flour, salt, and 1 tablespoon of oil into a bowl and add approximately 1 cup of cold water gradually to make a fairly soft dough. Knead with your hands for about 10 minutes. Cover and let rest for 15 or 20 minutes.

Divide the dough into small balls about the size of a walnut. Heat about 2 inches of oil to 375°F in a wok or deep heavy saucepan.

Roll out the balls on a floured work surface into 5-inch diameter circles. Work with one ball at a time and keep the rest covered with plastic wrap or a damp cloth. When the oil is hot, pick up the rolled-out puri with both hands and carefully lay it over the oil. Pat the puri very gently with the back of a slotted spoon as it floats on the oil; it should puff up like a ball in a few seconds. Turn it over gently and let it cook on the other side for 10 or 15 seconds. The puris should be a golden brown. Do not turn more than once or oil will seep inside. Drain on kitchen toweling.

Repeat with the remaining balls of dough. (You may roll out all the balls of dough in advance and keep them covered with a damp towel.) Serve at once, or keep warm in a covered dish and serve at room temperature.

Sherbanu's Puris

Preparation time: 50 minutes

Makes 14

1 cup whole wheat flour, plus extra for rolling
½ teaspoon salt
Vegetable oil for deep frying

Put the flour and salt in a bowl, gradually add ½ cup of water, and mix to a fairly soft dough. Knead for 5 minutes or longer, until soft but no longer sticky. Turn the dough onto a lightly floured surface. Roll with your hands until you have a long snake of dough, about ¾ inch in diameter.

Cut off a piece of dough about ¾ inch long and cover the remaining dough loosely with plastic wrap. Roll the cut-off piece of dough between your palms until it forms a small, neat ball. Coat it with flour, then roll it out until you have a small, flat patty about 3 inches in diameter. Continue cutting and shaping the dough in this way, always keeping the pieces of dough covered with plastic wrap when not being worked.

Heat about 2 inches of oil in a wok or large skillet until it is hot enough to brown a cube of bread in 30 seconds. Deep-fry the puris, one or two at a time, making sure you don't overcrowd the pan. Cook each batch for 2 or 3 minutes, until lightly browned, turning them once and splashing them with hot oil to make them puff up. Remove with a slotted spoon. Drain on paper towels before serving hot.

Hare Dhanya ki Roti

Coriander Roti

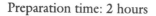

Preparation time: 2 hours

Makes 12

FOR THE FILLING:

> 6 fresh hot green chilies, seeded if desired, and coarsely chopped
> ½-inch piece of fresh ginger, peeled and coarsely chopped
> ½ teaspoon salt
> ¾ teaspoon ground coriander
> ¼ teaspoon ground cumin, roasted
> ¼ teaspoon turmeric
> 1 tablespoon besan (chick-pea) flour
> ½ bunch fresh coriander leaves and stems, trimmed of roots, washed
> and dried

FOR THE ROTIS:

> 1¾ cups whole wheat flour, plus extra for dusting the roti
> A pinch of salt
> 2 tablespoons vegetable oil, plus additional oil for brushing the roti
> Ghee (see page 299) or clarified butter, for frying

For the filling, put the chilies and ginger in a blender or food processor and grind to a paste. Add the salt, the ground coriander, cumin, turmeric, besan flour, and chopped fresh coriander, process together, and divide into 12 portions.

Coriander Roti (continued)

To make the roti dough, put the flour and salt in a bowl. Add the oil and rub it into the flour with your fingertips. Gradually add 6 to 7 tablespoons of water and mix to form a fairly soft ball. Knead for 4 or 5 minutes, until soft but not sticky. Divide the dough into 12 balls and cover with plastic wrap or a damp towel.

Taking one ball of dough at a time, dust it with flour and roll it out to a thin round about 5 inches in diameter. Brush with oil and place a portion of filling in the center. Fold the round over, bringing the edges together to seal. Roll again lightly, then brush with a little oil, fold in half again to form a triangle, and roll again to form a larger triangle with 5-inch sides. Take care not to let the filling out—just push it back in.

Melt some clarified butter or ghee on a griddle or in a heavy frying pan, and cook the roti for 1 or 2 minutes, turning once, until puffed up and lightly browned on both sides. Drain on paper towels before serving hot.

Ismail Merchant's Passionate Meals

THE CINEMA
AND THE
SWEETMEAT
SELLER

Sweets in India have a symbolic role. First, they have a religious significance, probably connected to the story of Krishna stealing the butter (from which many Indian sweets are made), and are given as offerings to the gods and goddesses. Also they are used as a gesture of goodwill and friendship, and guests to one's house are offered sweets immediately on arrival, with the saying "Let us sweeten your mouth." Business ventures are opened by the giving of sweets, as at the start of shooting a film. Even the tiniest

village in India, which may be composed of nothing more than a few shacks, will nevertheless have a halwai (a sweet-meat seller). When I was a child my pocket money had two destinations—the cinema and the halwai.

I am talking about Indian-style sweetmeats, and not desserts as they are known in the West. These are unlike any others in the world, intensely sweet and using quantities of milk, pistachios, almonds, sultanas (golden raisins), and sugar as the basic ingredients. I still love this type of sweet, and the recipes for carrot halva, Badam Paprh and Sheer Korma are some of my favorites, and are included in this book. The latter is an old family version of a famous recipe.

I also love fruit, and my other favorite desserts make use of the variety of tropical fruits that I knew growing up in Bombay as well as more common ones.

Badam Paprh

Almond Sweetmeat

Preparation time: 20–25 minutes, plus 6–8 hours drying

Serves 6–8

1¼ cups blanched almonds
½ cup firmly packed brown sugar
Confectioner's sugar

Pound and grind the almonds in a mortar and pestle until they become an oily mass. Alternatively, grind the almonds in a food processor, or chop them, then grind in batches in a blender until oily.

Add the brown sugar and knead the mixture thoroughly until it is very smooth and soft.

Divide the almond mixture into 6 or 8 portions and roll each into a ball. Lightly coat the balls with confectioner's sugar and use a rolling pin to roll each one into a thin round.

Leave the portions to dry on a muslin cloth for 6 to 8 hours.

Store up to 2 weeks, in between sheets of waxed paper, in an airtight container.

Amrit Pahl
Banana, Papaya, and Passion Fruit

Preparation time: 15–20 minutes

Serves 4–6

> 1 medium papaya
> 2 bananas
> 3 passion fruit
> ¾ cup milk
> 1½ teaspoons sugar, or to taste

Halve the papaya and remove the seeds. Peel and cut into 1-inch cubes. Peel the bananas and cut into ¼-inch slices. Halve the passion fruit and scoop out the pulp and seeds. Mix everything together with the milk and sugar, cool in the refrigerator, and serve.

Gajjar ka Halva
Carrot Halva with Raisins

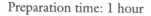

Preparation time: 1 hour

Serves 6

> A pinch of saffron
> ½ cup heavy cream
> 8 tablespoons (1 stick) butter, melted
> 1½ pounds carrots, peeled and grated (4½ cups)
> ¼ cup sugar
> ¼ cup raisins
> Seeds from 4 black cardamom pods
> ¼ cup slivered almonds
> 1 tablespoon rose water
> Heavy cream (optional)

Gently stir the saffron into 2 tablespoons of the cream. Gradually mix in the rest of the cream. The cream will take on the color of the saffron. Do not beat the mixture.

Melt the butter in a heavy saucepan over low heat. Add the grated carrots and stir to coat well.

Stir the sugar, raisins, and cardamom seeds into the carrot mixture.

Blend in the saffron and cream mixture; add the almonds. Sprinkle in the rose water, and cook for 30 to 40 minutes over low heat, stirring occasionally. The mixture will become a fairly dry, golden-brown mass.

Serve the halva with heavy cream poured over the top, if desired.

Sareefe ki Rabri
Frozen Custard Apple Cream

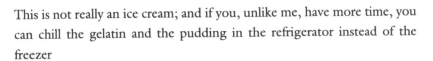

This is not really an ice cream; and if you, unlike me, have more time, you can chill the gelatin and the pudding in the refrigerator instead of the freezer

Preparation time: 25 minutes, plus 1–2 hours freezing

Serves 4–6

> 2 large custard apples (cherimoyas)
> ½ cup cold milk
> 1½ cups cold heavy cream
> 1½ teaspoons unflavored powdered gelatin
> A few drops of vanilla extract
> Confectioner's sugar, sifted

Spoon the pulp from the custard apples, discard the seeds and skin, and reserve.

Heat half the milk over very low heat, stirring with a wooden spoon. When hot, immediately pour the milk into a small bowl.

Sprinkle the gelatin over the hot milk and stir it briskly until it is dissolved. Put the mixture in the freezer until it just begins to set.

Meanwhile, combine the remaining ¼ cup of milk with 1 cup of the cream in a bowl; whisk until thick. Add the vanilla and sift in confectioner's sugar to taste.

Stir the custard apple pulp and thickened milk into the cream, and pour the mixture into a serving bowl. Place the pudding in the freezer for 1 to 2 hours.

Whisk the remaining ½ cup of cream until thick, decorate the pudding with it, and serve.

Aam Malai Shahrukh
Shahrukh's Mango Mousse

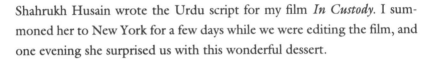

Shahrukh Husain wrote the Urdu script for my film *In Custody*. I summoned her to New York for a few days while we were editing the film, and one evening she surprised us with this wonderful dessert.

Preparation time: 10 minutes, plus chilling

Serves 6–8

> 1 (30-ounce) can of mango purée
> ¾ cup plus 1 tablespoon heavy cream
> 2 tablespoons sugar, or to taste (optional)
> 1½ envelopes unflavored gelatin

Empty the mango purée into a mixing bowl. Add ¾ cup of the cream and the sugar; mix very well. Dissolve the gelatin in ½ cup of boiling water and stir continuously until the water is clear. Pour the gelatin into the mango mixture and whisk it very quickly. Pour into a serving bowl, swirl a tablespoon of cream over the top, and refrigerate for 3 or 4 hours before serving.

Santre kie Chakle
Orange Wheels

◆

Preparation time: 10 minutes, plus chilling

Serves 4–6

6 large oranges

¼ cup sugar

2 tablespoons raisins

1 teaspoon ground nutmeg or cinnamon

¼ cup rose water

Juice of ½ lemon

2 tablespoons Grand Marnier, or other orange liqueur

Peel the oranges, carefully removing all the bitter white pith. Slice the oranges into 4 or 5 rounds and place them in a large shallow bowl.

Combine the sugar, raisins, nutmeg, rose water, lemon juice, and Grand Marnier, and pour the mixture over the orange wheels. Refrigerate for at least 2 hours.

Serve chilled, with some of the juice spooned over the oranges.

Aru Ka Salad

Peach Salad

Preparation time: 15 minutes

Serves 4–6

2 tablespoons rose water
4 teaspoons sugar
¼ teaspoon saffron
Juice of 1 lemon
8 fresh peaches, peeled, pitted, and sliced

In a serving bowl, combine the rose water, sugar, saffron, lemon juice, and ¼ cup water. Stir until the sugar is dissolved. Add the sliced peaches and stir them gently to coat with the liquid. Cool in the refrigerator and serve garnished with a few mint leaves, if desired.

Naaspati ka Murabba
Stewed Spiced Pears

Preparation time: 50 minutes

Serves 6

1½ lemons

12 firm ripe pears, peeled, cored, and cut into slices

1 cup sugar

1 teaspoon vanilla extract

3 cinnamon sticks

½ teaspoon ground cinnamon

3 ounces whole blanched almonds

Heavy cream (optional)

Trim the ends from the lemons, cut in half, and remove the seeds. Put the lemons in a food processor and blend until the lemons are a coarse paste.

Put the lemon paste in a large nonreactive saucepan with the pears, sugar, vanilla, cinnamon sticks, ground cinnamon, and the almonds. Cover and cook over medium-low heat for 40 minutes, stirring occasionally.

Remove the cinnamon sticks and serve the stewed pears with heavy cream, if desired.

Masaledar Ananas
Spiced Fresh Pineapple

◆

Preparation time: 10 minutes, plus chilling

Serves 4–6

  1 chilled pineapple
  Ground cinnamon OR freshly grated nutmeg

Peel and slice the pineapple.

  Place the slices on a serving dish and shake cinnamon or nutmeg over them.

NOTE: A little vanilla extract is another delightful addition to sprinkle over this simple, superb dessert.

Lal Ber Araqdar
Michael Fitzgerald's Strawberries

The American film producer Michael Fitzgerald grew up in Italy and cooks wonderful Italian food. He made this dessert for us one evening when he came to visit us in New York during the editing of *In Custody*.

Preparation time: 10 minutes, plus chilling

Wash strawberries in wine vinegar, cut them up, and put them in a bowl. Add 3 glasses of *good* red wine and a lot of sugar, then a squeeze of lemon juice. Leave the strawberries to sit for at least 3, and preferably 5, hours before serving.

Quartet Phal ka Salaad
Quartet Fruit Salad

❖

This is a dessert I created in Paris while we were on location for my film *Quartet,* starring Maggie Smith, Alan Bates, and Isabelle Adjani. For one of my Friday-night cast and crew parties I made this "cornucopia" of fruit salad, adding mint, red wine, lemon juice, and cinnamon to the fruit, and let people top it off with thick crème fraîche if they wished. For me, this feast of fruit helped me relive childhood experiences of shopping in the bazaars of Bombay.

Preparation time: 15 minutes, plus chilling

Serves 8–10

2 cups Beaujolais or other good red wine
4 teaspoons sugar
2 cinnamon sticks, broken into pieces
Juice of 4 lemons
2 pints ripe strawberries, hulled
4 kiwifruit, peeled and sliced
2 apples, cored and cubed
1 pound fresh sweet cherries, pitted
1½ pounds ripe peaches, peeled, pitted, and sliced
4 sprigs fresh mint, stems removed

Pour the wine into a large bowl. Add the sugar, cinnamon, and lemon juice. Prepare the rest of the ingredients in the order listed, stirring them immediately into the wine mixture.

Chill in the refrigerator for at least 2 hours before serving.

Crème Fraîche

Although Quartet Fruit Salad is perfect on its own, you can gild the lily by serving it with crème fraîche. Make it by mixing ½ cup sour cream with 1 cup heavy cream and leaving it in a warm room for 4 or 5 hours so the cream has a delicious sharpness. Cover and refrigerate until ready to use.

Shrikund

Festive Sweet Yogurt

◆

Preparation time: 10 minutes, plus draining and chilling

Serves 4–6

- 4 cups plain yogurt
- 1 ounce almonds, shelled
- 1 ounce unsalted pistachios, shelled
- ½ cup confectioner's sugar
- ½ teaspoon ground cardamom
- ¼ teaspoon saffron powder
- 2 tablespoons rose water

Line a colander with a large piece of muslin or several layers of cheese-cloth. Place the colander over a bowl. Pour the yogurt into the colander and let stand for 2 or 3 hours to drain off the excess water. The longer you drain it, the thicker the yogurt will be.

Meanwhile, drop the nuts in boiling water and blanch for 1 minute. Drain them well and rub off the skins with a cloth.

Turn the yogurt into a clean bowl. Add the sugar and mix the two together thoroughly.

Stir in the cardamom, saffron, and rose water. Pour the mixture into a glass serving bowl, and sprinkle the nuts over the top. Chill well and serve.

Kheer
Rice Pudding

Preparation time: 2–3 hours

Serves 4–6

   ¼ cup raw rice

   5 cups milk

   2 green cardamom pods, split

   1 tablespoon chopped almonds

   2 or 3 strands saffron

   1 tablespoon sugar, or to taste

Wash the rice 3 or 4 times and add to the milk in a saucepan, together with the cardamoms, almonds, and saffron strands. Simmer for 2 to 3 hours, uncovered, stirring frequently. Keep stirring in the skin that forms on the milk, as this gives the dish a rich, creamy texture. When the rice is well blended in with the milk, remove the pan from the heat and stir in the sugar. Serve hot or cold.

F e e r n i
Rice, Pistachio, and Almond Pudding

◈

Preparation time: about 25 minutes

Serves 4–6

1 cup sugar
5 cups fresh whole milk
¼ cup rice flour
¼ cup instant dried milk powder
6 to 8 blanched almonds, shelled
10 unsalted pistachios, shelled
A pinch of ground cardamom

Mix the sugar into the fresh whole milk, adding more if a sweeter pudding is desired, and heat in a heavy saucepan over medium-low heat. Meantime, stir the rice flour into 1 cup of water.

When the milk begins to boil, remove the pan from the heat and add the rice liquid, whisking vigorously to prevent lumps.

When the mixture is smooth, place it over medium-low heat, stir in the dried milk, and cook until thick, whisking occasionally.

Stir in the nuts and cardamom. Pour the mixture into small dessert bowls and cool. Serve at room temperature or lightly chilled.

Sheer Khorma
Pistachio-Almond Milk Pudding

◈

This is a very special pudding served on important feast days in Muslim households. On Id, the day we celebrate the end of Ramzan (the Muslim month of fasting), it is customary to eat something sweet in the morning after prayers. My mother would get up at four in the morning to prepare this special treat for us.

Preparation time: overnight soaking, plus about 40 minutes

Serves 12

3/4 pound unsalted pistachios, shelled
3 ounces almonds, shelled
2 ounces dried vermicelli (angel hair pasta)
1/2 cup (1 stick) butter
4 cups milk
3/4 cup cream
5 tablespoons sugar
1/2 teaspoon saffron

Place the pistachios and almonds in a bowl and add cold water to cover. Let them stand overnight, then drain and rub off the skins with a cloth.

Coarsely grind the nuts in a food processor or blender. Do not over-grind them.

Break the vermicelli into pieces about 4 inches long. Melt the butter in a large saucepan and add the vermicelli. Cook, stirring, until the vermicelli is nicely browned; be careful not to burn it.

Add the milk and cream and bring to the boil. Reduce the heat. Add the nut mixture, sugar and saffron. Simmer, stirring often, for about 15 minutes.

Serve warm, hot, or cold.

Seviyan

Vermicelli Pudding

Preparation time: 25 minutes

Serves 4–6

> 6 tablespoons butter
> 1 cup dried vermicelli (angel hair pasta)
> 1 heaping tablespoon finely chopped almonds
> 1½ teaspoons sugar
> Chopped almonds for garnish (optional)

Melt the butter in a saucepan. Add the vermicelli and gently cook for 5 to 7 minutes, stirring occasionally. Add the almonds, sugar, and ½ cup of water. Stir, cover the saucepan, and simmer for 7 to 10 minutes, or until all the water is absorbed. Serve hot, garnished with additional chopped almonds, if desired.

Sooji Halva
Semolina Dessert

❖

Preparation time: 20 minutes

Serves 4–6

1 cup (2 sticks) butter
1 cup sooji (semolina) or cream of wheat
2 tablespoons chopped nuts (almonds, pistachios, and/or walnuts)
¼ cup sugar
Seeds from 2 white or green cardamom pods
2 strands saffron

Melt the butter in a saucepan over low heat. Add the semolina and brown it slightly in the butter, stirring frequently for about 10 minutes. Add the chopped nuts.

In another saucepan, bring 2 cups of water to a boil. Add the sugar, cardamom seeds, and saffron. Over low heat, add the water slowly to the semolina mixture, stirring continuously. The consistency of this should be like a thick porridge. Serve hot.

You can prepare the semolina and water mixtures separately before dinner, and combine them just before serving.

Sample Menus
❖
Glossary
❖
Index
❖

Sample Menus

Unlike Western food, Indian cuisine has no hard and fast rules about which dishes are served together. Generally, it is mandatory to have rice, dal, and some form of bread at every meal, but otherwise you can choose any combination you feel like preparing. Also, an Indian meal is not served in separate courses. This may seem odd, especially as meat and fish can be served at the same meal, but it works because the spices are complementary.

Here are some suggestions:

1

VEAL WITH MUSTARD AND DILL SAUCE
ROAST CHICKEN WITH PARSLEY AND MUSTARD
KEEMA MATAR
ZUCCHINI WITH WHOLE GREEN PEPPERCORNS
BASMATI PILAF
PARATHAS (BREAD)

PEACH SALAD

2

PEPPER CHICKEN
GREEN BEANS
MIXED DAL
PLAIN BASMATI RICE
GREEN SALAD

MANGO MOUSSE

3

KOFTA
SPICY STEWED CAULIFLOWER AND POTATOES
SPINACH, TOMATOES, AND MOONG DAL
GREEN PEA PILAF
CUCUMBER RAITA

SPICED FRESH PINEAPPLE

4

MUSTARD SHRIMP
BROCCOLI IN GARLIC-LEMON BUTTER
SAFFRON PILAF
LEMON LENTILS
PURIS (BREAD)

STEWED SPICED PEARS

Glossary

Asafetida

A brown, somewhat smelly resin used in small quantities in Indian cooking partly for its flavor, mostly as a digestive.

Basmati

A long-grain rice, slender, delicate, and naturally perfumed. Before cooking, it must be picked over and washed in several changes of water.

Caraway Seeds

Gathered from a plant native to both Asia and Europe, this spice is used mostly in north Indian cooking. It's best to bruise the seeds a little in a mortar and pestle just before using them to bring out their flavor.

Cardamom

This aromatic spice comes in two basic types, the smaller pale green or white pods and the larger black or "wild" pods. Sometimes the tiny black seeds are removed from the pods and crushed to use in cooking, but I usually use the whole pods in my recipes; it's easier. People just leave them on the side of their plate.

Chana Dal (or gram dal)

Hulled and split peas that are deep yellow in color and do not need presoaking.

Chilies, red and green

These vary in heat and spiciness, the red ones being dried and the fresh ones green. They vary in size from two to four inches, and contain many white seeds, some or all of which you can leave in, if you like spicier food.

Cinnamon This comes from the paper-thin bark of a tree, which, when dry, curls into sticks. They have so much more flavor than ground cinnamon that I use the sticks whole or broken whenever I want the flavor of cinnamon in my dishes.

Continental Masoor Whole, greenish-brown lentils, flat and oval-shaped; they do not need pre-soaking.

Coriander This herb from the parsley family is used in two ways in Indian cooking—fresh and green (when it's also known as cilantro) and the dry brown seeds. Both have very different tastes.

Garam Masala An aromatic mixture of ground spices, such as cardamom, cloves, cinnamon, cumin, and nutmeg, meant to "heat up" the body.

Fenugreek Both the dried leaves and the seeds are used in Indian cooking—each has very different properties.

Ghee Clarified butter, totally free of all milk solids, with a nutty taste that comes from long simmering.

Ginger (or adrak) The fresh ginger used in Indian cooking is the knobby growth on the root, not the root itself. Sometimes I don't bother, but its thin skin should really be peeled before grating or chopping, especially if using it in a purée. Rarely if ever do I use dried ground ginger.

Ground Red Pepper Cayenne or chili powder, also called "red powder" in Indian groceries; is basic to Indian cooking.

Gur (or jaggery)	A form of raw lump sugar, generally honey-brown in color.
Hava Masala	A mixture of ginger, garlic, and green chilies.
Kabli Chana	Unhulled and beige in color, these chick-peas need overnight soaking before cooking.
Kala Chana	Small brown or black chick-peas, they require long presoaking and cooking to become tender.
Masoor	Brown, Indian lentils, smaller than continental masoor, they do not require presoaking.
Masoor Dal	Tiny, salmon-pink, split masoor that have been hulled and do not need presoaking.
Mung Beans (or hari dal)	Small, dark green, and slightly cylindrical, they need two to four hours' soaking before cooking, but if oversoaked they will sprout and become mung bean sprouts.
Moong Dal	Light yellow, rectangular, and split, these mung beans do not need to be soaked before cooking.
Moong Dal Chilka	Split mung beans, green on one side and pale on the other, they do not need presoaking.
Mustard Seeds (or sarson)	Both yellow and black mustard seeds are used in Indian cooking. I prefer the black ones because of the way they look in a dish, but yellow ones do nicely. The seeds are also made into a fairly spicy oil and, of course, into prepared mustards.
Saffron	This is sold dried, both as yellow-red threads and powdered. It's expensive in either form, but only a little of this very important spice is needed. Many sweets, rice pilafs, and chicken dishes would pine for lack of it.

Sev	Crisp chick-pea flour noodles.
Tamarind	Sour brown pulp of the tamarind pod, purchased in cake form. To use it, follow instructions in recipe, or break off a lump and cover with hot water (for 1 pound of pulp use 2 cups of water). Let it stand overnight in a nonmetallic bowl—or just simmer it for 10 minutes, or until it softens, if you're in a rush. Squeeze the pulp with your fingers or force it through a sieve together with the soaking liquid. Discard the solids.
Toor Dal (or arhar dal)	Dull and yellow-colored lentils. Hulled, split, a little larger than chana dal, they need presoaking before cooking.
Turmeric	Part of the ginger family, it is a mild, earthy dried ground spice that makes many of the Indian foods yellow. It is used as a digestive and antiseptic.
Urid (or black matpe)	Small and black, similar to mung beans, they need presoaking before cooking.
Urid Dal	Off-white, hulled, washed, and split, they need presoaking before cooking.

Index

bhuna phasli, 197
biryani, 142–44
bread, 262–72
    coriander roti, 271–72
    English paratha, 268
    flat, 265
    fried wheat, 264
    parathas, 267
    potato, 266
    puris, 269
    puris, Sherbanu's, 270
brinjal pullao, 137
broccoli:
    in garlic-lemon butter, 60
    ginger soup, 35
bundi raita, 21

caper and mustard salmon, 229–30
caraway:
    onion potato salad, 96
    red pepper roast chicken, 147
    roast lamb with ginger and, 179–80
cardamom and coriander rice, 136
carrot:
    and cauliflower achar, Sherbanu's, 260
    halva with raisins, 277
    salad, 47
    soup, Claverack, 36–37
cashew and lamb stew, 192–94
cauliflower:
    and carrot achar, Sherbanu's, 260
    pickle, 258
    spicy stewed potatoes and, 94–95
    stewed tomatoes and, 61
chahar dal, 111
challia dahi, 65
chapati, 265
chapli kabab, 205
cheese:
    green peas with, 72
    homemade, 76
    paneer with cumin, 77
    spinach with, 75–76
    toasts with mustard seeds, 24
chicken, 145
    baked, 158
    biryani, 142–44
    cacciatore, Roberto Silvi's, 165–66
    chili and parsley stuffing for, 148
    coriander, 162
    with cumin, 163

curry, spicy, 156–57
Duncan, 160–61
hot and honey-roasted, 151
lemon, ginger, and chili stuffing for,
    149
livers baked in spicy mustard, 168
livers baked in spicy yogurt, 167
pancake and chutney stuffing for, 148
pepper, 155
red pepper-caraway roast, 147
roast, with parsley and mustard, 150
spicy, 159
tandoori, Dan's, 164
tomato, 154
yogurt, I, 152
yogurt, II, 153
chick-pea(s):
    black, with gram flour sauce, 122–23
    dal, 104
    potatoes and, 120–21
    whole black, 119
chili(es):
    fresh corn with, 62–63
    lemon, and ginger stuffing for chicken,
        149
    and parsley stuffing for poultry, 148
    tomato salad, 53
chilla aur chutni-walla murgh, 148
chives, boiled potatoes with scallions and,
    88
chuqandar Monesh, 49
chutney and pancake stuffing for chicken,
    148
chutneys, 246–61
    mango, 254
    mango relish, 259
    mint and coriander, 250
    sweet peach, 257
    tomato, 253
    tomato, Parveen's, 251–52
    see also pickles
Claverack ka khas gajar shorba, 36–37
coconut:
    dumplings in vegetable stew, 81–83
    lobster, 239
    and raisin raita, 17
    sauce, mackerel in, 222
    sauce, spicy, 223
cod(fish):
    in coriander sauce, 220
    curry, spicy, 234–35

Ismail Merchant's Passionate Meals

Ismail Merchant's Passionate Meals